Blues of a Lifetime

Blues of a Lifetime:

The Autobiography of Cornell Woolrich

Edited by
Mark T. Bassett

Bowling Green State University Popular Press
Bowling Green, Ohio 43403

Contents

Introduction

The world of Cornell Woolrich is both colder and more romantic than that of the "hard-boiled" writers Dashiell Hammett, Raymond Chandler, and James M. Cain. Like his contemporaries, Woolrich knew how to ensnare readers within a starkly chiseled maze of corruption. He too was familiar with a landscape traversed by honor-bound detectives, sexual criminals, and inept policemen. Yet in most of his haunting suspense novels, Woolrich's prose inspires visions of "the blues." A solitary figure, trapped beneath the dark heaven of an indifferent universe, aches for love but is doomed to die alone. It is an inevitable and devastating fate that awaits Woolrich's characters, yet they seem compelled to struggle until the ninth hour arrives. And with these ill-fated heroes, the reader is held in suspense, hoping in vain that character does not determine destiny.

Cornell Woolrich was, as the French critic Francis Lacassin notes, "the king of the thrillers" (41). "At his best," Ellery Queen once remarked, "Woolrich projects a powerful atmosphere of fear, shock and violence, and usually his stories end with a whiplash of surprise" (12). To biographer Francis M. Nevins, Jr., Woolrich is "the Poe of the twentieth century and the poet of its shadows" (110). To novelist Anthony Boucher, he was a "black magician" for whom murder was ordinary, a mere "noonday devil," and whose fiction revealed the "potential terror" of an otherwise banal day (125).

His greatest works have something of poetry or drama in them as well. Therefore, he offered a young Harlan Ellison "a treasurehouse of twists and turns in plotting, elegant writing style, misdirection, mood, setting and suspense" (38). Barry N. Malzberg, who worked briefly as Woolrich's agent, marvels that although Woolrich's characters are "rendered with great sensitivity," they remind us of the protagonists in classical Greek tragedy, frequently entering the scene "so damaged" that their lives seem a "vast anticlimax to central and terrible events [occurring] long before the incidents of the story" (321, 332). And Francis Lacassin writes, "He was a narrator of tragic tales, a psychologist, a moralist, also a poet... And as a painter, Woolrich was the impressionist of the detective novel" (41).

Among the twenty-two novels and more than 200 short stories, published under his own name or under the pen-names "William Irish" and "George Hopley," Woolrich's masterpieces include "The Night Reveals" (1936); "Three O'Clock" (1938); *The Bride Wore Black* (1940); *The Black Curtain* (1941); *Black Alibi* (1942); *Phantom Lady* (1942); "Rear Window" (1942); *The Black Angel* (1943); *The Black Path of Fear* (1944); *Deadline at Dawn* (1944); *Night Has a Thousand Eyes* (1945); *Waltz into Darkness* (1947); *I Married a Dead Man* (1948); *Rendezvous in Black* (1948); and "Too Nice a Day to Die" (1965). At the height of his career, during the 1940s, while French readers were snapping up copies of Woolrich's "black series" in translation, his motifs and moods began to dominate those black-and-white American thrillers that we now call *film noir* (literally, "black film"). Woolrich reached a broader audience via film, then radio, then television. By his death in 1968, more of Woolrich's fiction had been translated into *film noir* than that of any other writer.

In the early 1980s, as a testimony to his long and influential career, Ballantine Books reissued most of his major works in a uniform paperback series. Thanks to the efforts of Francis M. Nevins, Jr., many of the early works have also been reprinted during the last two decades. And in 1988, his definitive study *Cornell Woolrich: First You Dream, Then You Die*, published by Mysterious Press, received an Edgar Allan Poe Award from the Mystery Writers of America. Clearly, the works and the life of Cornell George Hopley-Woolrich have grasped the imagination of mystery fans for decades, even though the author's name is not immediately recognizable in the typical American household.

Part of this relative anonymity stems from the banality of Woolrich's adult life. As he explained in 1944,

I have led a completely uneventful life, as far as outward incident is concerned, so it is extremely difficult to find enough substance for a biography....

I live in a hotel in New York. I have lived in hotels all my life; I was brought up in them even as a child. I have traveled now and then, but I suspect it was wasted effort. A hotel room is a hotel room, whether the place outside your windows is called New York, Paris, London or whatnot; they all look alike.

This sort of life would be fatal to a writer trying to write realistically; that is, of the world as it is. You don't see anything of it, you don't know anything of it. Fortunately I am a writer of the imagination. What I write is entertainment-fiction, that hasn't a great deal to do with the world as it actually is. So I can write a story of Paris in a New York hotel room, or a story of New York in a Paris hotel room equally successfully. Neither one is Paris, and neither one is New York, but if they entertain, they've made the grade. And that, I think, is about all; both of my philosophy and of this autobiographical effort. (see Furman 410)

Even the autobiography that Woolrich left unpublished at his death, *Blues of a Lifetime*, is sketchy and contradictory. When read in connection with what little is indeed known of his life, the autobiography portrays Woolrich as a shadowy figure. We know almost as much about him from reading his fiction as we do from studying other evidence.

We know from the first section of *Blues of a Lifetime* that Woolrich spent part of his youth in Mexico, living with his father after his parents' separation. And the Mexican Revolution featured strongly in his memories of his childhood. He once wrote to Stanley Kunitz, "Nearly every second night at dinner, lights would fail, which meant either that Villa had captured the town from Carranza, or Carranza had captured it from Villa.... Every time there was a new 'triumphal entry,' the schools would close down for a day or two, until the sporadic shooting had quieted down." Yet where and when did Woolrich live in Mexico? What was his father's occupation? What became of the elder Woolrich? All one can do is study the available evidence and draw conjectures.

During 1913-1915, it seems, Woolrich and his father must have lived in one of the Laguna District villages, near the dams on the river Naza. Several accounts of the effect of revolution on those towns echo Woolrich's description of it. Gómez Palacio is the most likely site, since it was strategically located near Torreón, a larger village that was coveted for its political, economic and military importance. Patrick A. O'Hea, author of *Reminiscences of the Mexican Revolution*, remembers the "kaleidoscopic changes of the Mexican revolutionary struggle... alternately advancing and receding, flaring up and dying down, with periods of tranquillity as the line of conflict receded from us" (40). According to O'Hea, the fighting

invariably involved the capture of, or retreat from, our town.... We of Gómez Palacio always knew that we would be the first to be attacked and the last to be relinquished.... In a cycle of twelve months reckoned between the latter part of 1913 and through some nine months of 1914, we were taken and re-taken, in armed assault and street-to-street fighting, no less than six times. (133)

Witness also the following account of a 1915 raid on Gómez Palacio, published by Elías L. Torres in *Twenty Episodes in the Life of Pancho Villa.*

A night of serenade...the small public garden of Gómez Palacio was filled to bursting with people strolling along its walks dimly lighted by electric light bulbs. In the center was the kiosk where the town band loosed the strains of the most popular music of those days....

The band played the last selection at ten o'clock sharp and little by little the plaza began to be deserted; the hawkers packed up their wares, the shops closed their doors, lights began going out in the saloons and the city quietly slept, with that blessed quiet of the provinces when there is absolute trust, when there is not the least fear of the fury of war.

Shortly after three o'clock in the morning an avalanche of horsemen poured into the town, firing shots and opening the doors of the shops with rifle-butts and blows....

Then, all the horrors of frightful surprise attacks: dead, wounded, rifled, unbridled drunkenness, women crying for help while being dragged up on a horse, children weeping lost in the streets, and an infernal chorus of barking dogs also terrified by the invading fury.

Gómez Palacio, at the break of day, presented the aspect of a man beaten into wakefulness, showing in his gaze the shock, the astonishment of such a rude shaking. (38-40)

The passage reads as if it belonged in a Woolrich novel, lending credence to Lacassin's assumption that the emotional turmoil of the Revolution had a lasting impact on him and his fiction. Yet to draw these conclusions requires a leap of faith, since documentary evidence is scant.

Other events in Woolrich's life are equally mysterious. No one knows exactly when or why he moved from his father's flat in Mexico to live with his mother in New York at his maternal grandfather's home. Even though we know that he attended Columbia University during 1921-1926, no one can say quite why he failed to graduate, nor exactly the motive for launching upon a writing career. Were his parents ever divorced? Did his father know of his success as a suspense writer? What is the truth behind his unconsummated marriage to actress Gloria Blackton? Why did he insist, after almost 30 years of life in a hotel room shared with his mother, that he be buried in her doubled-sized crypt after his death? These questions, as fully as they can be answered, are among the enigmas addressed by Francis M. Nevins, Jr., in *Cornell Woolrich*.

The evidence shows that Woolrich was on a seven-month vacation in Canada in 1961 when he sketched the outline for the opening section of *Blues of a Lifetime*, on stationery from the Royal Alexandra Hotel in Winnipeg. By December 1966, he had abandoned the work, after writing only five full drafts of the projected six sections. The sixth "story," whose subject is unknown to us, may never have been titled, outlined, or drafted. Woolrich scholars therefore face yet another unanswerable mystery: what would have been its focus? Could it have assessed his career? Summarized his fictional themes or life philosophy? Described his trips to Canada, Europe, Central and South America? Lamented his failed marriage? Characterized his relationship with his father? Revealed the nature of his reading life? Any of those subjects would have been welcome, since they are largely neglected in *Blues of a Lifetime*, however suitable they might seem for an autobiography.

Meanwhile, the typescript for *Blues of a Lifetime*, found by his executors in a safety deposit box, was accompanied by a cryptic note:

I have not written this for it to be well-written, nor read by anyone else; I have written it for myself alone. This is the way it was; this is the way it has to be told. It makes me blue to look back at the past. But I want to look back *Ice* more, before it's gone forever.

The note, which provides only a few clues to his methods and intentions in writing the autobiography, is puzzling. If Woolrich did not intend for the work to be published one day, why did he ensure that it was salvaged for posterity, along with only a handful of typescripts of his suspense fiction?

Clearly intended as an accounting, before death, *Blues of a Lifetime* is a moody collection of "personal stories," sometimes dark, but also antic. Writing them probably made him "blue," just as so many popular melodies color his best fiction. Yet the volume explains his life, not only "the way it was," but "the way it has to be told." To Woolrich, the notions are synonymous, not contradictory. Doesn't he write a similar belief in the second chapter of *Blues of a Lifetime*: "That's all there are, are our images of things. There are no realities. There are only the hundred different approximations of reality that are our images of it, no two the same, from man to man, from case to case, from place to place" (57-58).

Obviously, Woolrich was taken with the sentiments of his beloved dancer Isadora Duncan, who opens her own autobiography with these words: "Nothing seems to exist save in the imagination.... How can we write the truth about ourselves? Do we even know it? There is the vision our friends have of us; the vision we have of ourselves, and the vision our lover has of us. Also the vision our enemies have of us— and all these visions are different." And, appropriately, Woolrich penned this phrase from Ben Hecht's dark story of a dancer, "Spectre of the Rose," as his "personal motto": "I am unfit for living. I am fit only for art" (recorded in Woolrich's record book).

Reader, do not hope for "the unvarnished truth" in Woolrich's autobiography. He opts instead for a transcendent, a metaphorical truth in relating these personal stories. For Woolrich, as for Joan Didion, the literal facts have become less important than their symbolic meaning. Woolrich himself might have written these words, from Didion's famous essay "On Keeping a Notebook": "My approach to daily life ranges from the grossly negligent to the merely absent-minded.... Perhaps it never did snow that August in Vermont;...and perhaps no one else felt the ground hardening and summer already dead even as we pretended to bask in it, but that was how it felt to me, and it might have snowed, could have snowed, did snow" (12). After reading Woolrich's *Blues of a Lifetime*, one should join Jorge Luis Borges in thinking, as he urges the readers of the short story "Emma Zunz" to believe, that "actually, the story *was* incredible, but it impressed everyone because substantially it was true. True was Emma Zunz' tone, true was her shame, true was her hate. True also was the outrage she had suffered: only the circumstances were false, the time, and one or two proper names" (137).

We tend to overlook such concerns while reading "Remington Portable NC69411," the opening section of *Blues of a Lifetime*. When there is action in this chapter, the people and events are private, rather than public, making their veracity difficult to determine. It seems perfectly plausible that Woolrich might have borrowed a friend's typewriter during 1924, or that he was initiated into sexuality with the tutoring of such a friend. Yet, because much of the chapter is interwoven with Woolrich's thoughts, memories, impressions and opinions, the need to validate truth is less weighty here perhaps than in later chapters.

In contrast, the second story, titled "The Poor Girl," turns out to have a real-life basis in an incident reported in the *New York Times*. The "truth" beneath this surface will be offered in a note from the editor, so as not to spoil the effect of Woolrich's story. For despite the fact that no mention of the name Cornell Woolrich is made in the court records summarized in the notes, the character Vera Gaffney appears to have been inspired by Woolrich's friendship with a "model" named Catherine Bennett. Other details of the tale will elude verification—the existence of the boxer friend Frank Van Craig, the visit to Vera's parents, the party for Janet Lambert, the climactic block party, the black sedan. And a similar rewriting of the "truth" appears to have taken place in the fourth section, "President Eisenhower's Speech," an explanation of which is also to be found in the editor's notes.

There are two more stories in *Blues of a Lifetime*: "Even God Felt the Depression" (about Woolrich's loss of faith) and "The Maid Who Played the Races" (about fame and obscurity, while he was staying temporarily in a Seattle hotel). Perhaps these chapters too have undercurrents of reality, beneath a carefully composed surface—artfully arranged for the sake of those readers Woolrich claimed not to be writing for. In the end it seems that he might like to tell the truth, although "telling it slant," in the style of Emily Dickinson. And perhaps this is in fact the way his life story "has to be told." Writing, romance, despair, mother, loneliness. Isn't that all we know—and need to know—about Cornell Woolrich?

* * * * *

The typescript of *Blues of a Lifetime*, along with a carbon copy, is archived in the Cornell Woolrich collection at the Rare Book and Manuscripts Collection, Butler Library, Columbia University. Woolrich's will specified that his entire estate (with a few minor omissions) go to Columbia University for the purpose of establishing the Claire Attalie Woolrich Memorial Scholarship Fund, awarded to students in journalism.

At the time of his death in 1968, this estate was worth approximately $850,000.

The typescript and carbon contain relatively few revisions. These are typically in holograph (handwriting) and easily legible, although some are not fully transferred from one copy to the other. In preparing this "clear text" for publication, I have respected such revisions, regardless of their source in the original papers.

In the process of examining the edited typescripts (also at Columbia University) of *Waltz into Darkness* and *Night Has a Thousand Eyes* for a conference paper to the Popular Culture Association, I made several important observations. Woolrich's editors—in each case—made countless corrections to his spelling and punctuation, for which the author was evidently grateful. His marginal comments illustrate that he yielded to his editors on these points. Therefore, in editing *Blues of a Lifetime*, I have not hesitated to adopt standard usage in regard to hyphens, quotation marks, parentheses, and commas. However, Woolrich's fiction is often marked stylistically by the occasional comma splice, and he coins new compound nouns on nearly every page of most of his novels. Readers will find, as a result, that these two minor "violations" of modern usage have sometimes been allowed to stand.

The edited typescripts of these two published works also reveal that Woolrich often bowed to editorial decisions concerning structure. Now and then, Woolrich's editors recommended that a lengthy passage be condensed (a revision that Woolrich claims, on page 11, would have aided some of his early fiction). In other instances, the editors would insist on minor rearrangements in order to maintain the logic of a police procedure.

Although I have not felt it a wise choice to make such alterations to *Blues of a Lifetime*, readers should be aware that the editor has sometimes employed these and similar devices in favor of concision and clarity. In one instance where I felt compelled to condense a particularly long-winded passage containing little action, this decision has been so noted in the footnotes. Occasionally, the breaks that organize Woolrich's prose have been slightly altered by the editor as well.

Most of the footnotes are intended as supplements to the text of *Blues of a Lifetime* in cases where Woolrich indeed seems to have "written it for myself alone." Proper nouns are identified whenever possible. The findings of other researchers have been acknowledged where it was useful. If any errors have crept into these footnotes, may I ask the reader's forgiveness.

Of course it is, first of all, important to thank Cornell Woolrich for leaving some of his memories and moods to us in the form of *Blues of a Lifetime*. And, as editor, I have others to thank for their many contributions to my work, including Francis M. Nevins, Jr., whose

research and support have been invaluable—along with the courtesies
and various offerings of Barry N. Malzberg, Donald Yates, Burton L.
Lilling, Jr., Pat Browne, George Cooper, Bernard Crystal, Mary M.
Lago, the Iowa State University research grant programs, the Wichita State
University research grant programs, the Popular Culture Association (esp.
the Caucus for Mystery and Detective Fiction), James Lee Burke, the
Missouri Philological Association, William McCarthy, and Dale Ross.

Works Cited

Borges, Jorge Luis. "Emma Zunz." *Labyrinths: Selected Stories and Other Writings.*
    Trans. Donald A. Yates and James E. Irby. New York: New Directions, 1962.
Boucher, Anthony. Introduction. *The Bride Wore Black,* by Cornell Woolrich. 1940;
    rpt. New York: Collier, 1964.
Didion, Joan. "On Keeping a Notebook." *Holiday* December 1966: 10-12, 19-20.
Duncan, Isadora. *My Life.* Garden City, NY: Garden City Publishing, 1927.
Ellison, Harlan. "Introduction: Blood/Thoughts." *No Roses, No Windows.* New
    York: Ace, 1983.
Furman, A.L., ed. *Third Mystery Companion.* New York: Gold Label, 1945.
Kunitz, Stanley. First Supplement to *Twentieth Century Authors.* New York: Wilson,
    1955.
Lacassin, Francis. "Cornell Woolrich: Psychologist, Poet, Painter, Moralist" (1974).
    Trans. Mark T. Bassett. *Clues: A Journal of Detection* 8.2 Fall/Winter 1987:
    41-78.
Malzberg, Barry N. "Woolrich." *The Fantastic Stories of Cornell Woolrich.* Eds.
    Charles G. Waugh and Martin H. Greenberg. Carbondale: Southern Illinois
    UP, 1985. 299-327. [Also in Malzberg, *The Engines of the Night* (Garden City,
    NY: Doubleday, 1982).]
Nevins, Francis M., Jr. *Cornell Woolrich: First You Dream, Then You Die.* New
    York: Mysterious Press, 1988.
O'Hea, Patrick A. *Reminiscences of the Mexican Revolution.* México City: Editorial
    Fournier, 1966.
Queen, Ellery. Introduction. *The Ten Faces of Cornell Woolrich.* New York: Simon
    & Schuster, 1965.
Torres, Elías L. "Villa's Vengeance" (Episodio VIII). *Twenty Episodes in the Life
    of Pancho Villa.* Trans. Sheila M. Ohlendorf. Austin: Encino Press, 1973.
Woolrich, Cornell. *Black Alibi.* 1942; rpt. New York: Ballantine, 1982.
_____ *The Black Angel.* 1943; rpt. New York: Ballantine, 1982.
_____ *The Black Curtain.* 1941; rpt. New York: Ballantine, 1982.
_____ *The Black Path of Fear.* 1944; rpt. New York: Ballantine, 1982.
_____ *The Bride Wore Black.* 1940; rpt. New York: Ballantine, 1984.
_____ *Deadline at Dawn.* 1944; rpt. New York: Ballantine, 1983. [Orig. publ. as
    by William Irish.]
_____ *I Married a Dead Man.* 1948; rpt. New York: Ballantine, 1983. [Orig. publ.
    as by William Irish.]
_____ *Night Has a Thousand Eyes.* 1945; rpt. New York: Ballantine, 1983. [Orig.
    publ. as by George Hopley.]

_____ "The Night Reveals." 1936; rpt. in *The Ten Faces of Cornell Woolrich*. New York: Simon & Schuster, 1965. [Orig. publ. as by William Irish.]

_____ *Phantom Lady*. 1942; rpt. New York: Ballantine, 1982. [Orig. publ. as by William Irish.]

_____ "Rear Window." 1942; rpt. in *Rear Window and Four Short Novels*. New York: Ballantine, 1984. [Orig. publ. as by William Irish.]

_____ *Rendezvous in Black*. 1948; rpt. New York: Ballantine, 1982.

_____ "Three O'Clock." 1938; rpt. in *Rear Window and Four Short Novels*. New York: Ballantine, 1984. [Orig. publ. as by William Irish.]

_____ "Too Nice a Day to Die." 1965; rpt. in *Nightwebs: A Collection of Stories by Cornell Woolrich*. Ed. Francis M. Nevins, Jr. New York: Harper, 1971.

_____ *Waltz into Darkness*. 1947; rpt. New York: Ballantine, 1983. [Orig. publ. as by William Irish.]

Blues of a Lifetime
(Personal Stories)

by
Cornell Woolrich

Each of us, alone, unaided, of his own powers, must unravel the riddle...before death, or else part in despair.

Buddenbrooks, Thomas Mann

I
Remington Portable NC69411

The first section of Blues of a Lifetime *is particularly valuable for Woolrich's biographers. It is the episodic account of his motives, while a student at Columbia University, for writing his first novel. From time to time, the chapter glances at key experiences from Woolrich's youth. Here readers can learn about his reactions to his grandfather's death; Woolrich's first sexual encounter; his first publication; his writing habits; his first opera; his fatalism; and his hollow craving for companionship, joy and meaning in life.*

More loose, structurally, than the other chapters in Blues of a Lifetime, *this nostalgic opening "story" contains passages of great beauty and a typical Woolrichian twist at the end. Most of the action takes place in New York City during the months of March through September 1925, when Woolrich was 21.*

We first met, you and I, a long time ago. You looked different then, I looked different then.[1] Who wouldn't look different, that long a time ago? I can give you the exact date, year-date, if you want. I've a very good head for dates, a very good memory for them.[2] I've seen so many of them go by. But no—dates are cold, rigid, precision-like things, dates are for calendars, not for a warm story, not for a brotherly-love story, like yours and mine.

This was a mating if there ever was one. A life-long partnership, a fellowship, a combine, of flesh and of thin steel casing, of fingertips and of keys, of mind and of agilely responsive mechanism: lower case that turned to upper at a tap, upper that turned back to lower at another tap; asterisks, apostrophes, parentheses, quotation marks, single quotation marks to go within the double, hyphens and colons and commas that flashed up like sparks, and like sparks dimmed again, left behind in the onrush; the warning bell that stopped each line in its tracks; the indentation brake that made each line start even with the ones before; the seldom-used dollar sign and the never-used ¼- and ½-symbols that looked so unreal somehow when they did crop up, perhaps due to that very lack of use; the color-lever that could turn the ribbon from black to red (but only if the ribbon was half red already, and I never used one of those hybrids, those bastards, in my life).

3

And into this transformer, this reagent, went streams of thought and dramatic highspots and narrative stretches printed invisibly on the retina of the mind, and out of it they came printed visibly now in black type on white paper, in order that they could be conveyed to others, and taken in again to the retinas of other minds. From privacy out into publicity, and then back into privacy again.

But why? Where the need for it? We're not concerned with that here. That's a question no painter of pictures, no writer of words, can fairly be asked to answer.

He must do it, that's all he knows.

The love of a man for his machine. I never loved women much, I guess. Only three times, that I'm fully aware of. And each time I got more or less of a kick in the jaw, so there wasn't much incentive to go ahead trying more frequently. The first time it was just puppy love, but it ended disastrously for at least one of us, through no fault of mine.[3] The second time, somebody else married her, and it was only after it happened that I realized I wished it hadn't. The third time, I married her, and it was only after it happened that I realized I wished it hadn't.

I was born to be solitary, and I liked it that way. Some are, and some do. And all the many times, probably the hundreds of times, I've sat alone at a table somewhere, a drink out in front of me, during the late hours, the closing hours, holding my face against my hand and staring pensively before me because I had no one to go home to and nowhere to go home to, it was just a sentimental "act" (meaning a piece of theatrical stage-business), a melancholy pose for my own benefit, and deep down inside I knew that I was lying to myself, and that I wouldn't have had it otherwise, and that if someone had been waiting somewhere for me with open arms at that very moment, I would have turned and run in the opposite direction as fast as I could. Probably carrying my *weltschmerz* libation along in one hand. To sit down in some other, safer place and start my wistful brooding all over again.

For if anyone ever entered my life for more than a few days or a few weeks at a time, the doors would remorselessly swing together and shut them out again, just as though they worked on spring hinges. And then inevitably, the next following New Year's Eve, I'd resurrect them in memory and toast them and mourn their passing. I cherished my solitude; I liked to have something to lament. And more pertinently, it made a wonderful background for my work. It sat well on me while I was young. Then when I no longer was quite so young, it sat less well. By that time it wasn't always altogether a fantasy any more, a self-imposed wishful state, either; but I could no longer tell the one from the other by then, anyway. The self-imposed had become the extraneously imposed, and loneliness was real.

Everyone can claim credit for at least one thing, one good point. Everyone has one. And I too can claim credit for at least one thing: self-honesty. I've never lied in all my life, not to anyone else, and not to myself. And that is why, though these pages may be boring, though these pages may be fatuous and unremarkable, these pages will at least be truthful.[4]

This is how it came about, this is how I came to own and have you:

One day in early spring, in March, I came back from my last class of the day late in the afternoon, and as I put my key into the door, I happened to glance aside into one of the narrow mirror-strips that bordered each side of it. The house had been designed when ornamentation and amenity of structure counted for something. The door was not flush with the street, but was an inner door set back within a four-square, mosaic-floored little vestibule, hence the mirror trim.

It was just a casual glance first, then something made me look a second time to make sure I had seen what I thought I had the first time. I had. The whites of my eyes had turned noticeably yellow.[5]

I was surprised and I wondered what it was, but there didn't seem to be anything I could do about it, so I shrugged it off and went on inside.

I was a college junior at the time, and the house, which was my grandfather's, was just a short walk from the campus.[6] I was living in it in order to cut down on the expense of taking a room in one of the dorms. My father had been sending the money to pay for my tuition-fees up from Mexico City, but the conversion into American dollars put a pretty bad crimp into it, and I surmised he wasn't doing too well just then, although he wouldn't admit the fact (at least not to me), so whatever corners could be cut in the costly and lengthy process of turning a boy into a man, education-wise, were all to the good.[7]

By the following day the coloration, or I suppose discoloration, in my eyes had grown more distinct. They were now a glaring saffron, and not very lovely to look at. I still couldn't do anything but wonder about it.

Then the skin of my face started to take on the same tinge. First the color of lemon peel, then down the chromatic scale until it had reached a full-bodied, repulsive orange.

I didn't have the nerve to show myself outside the door. I experimented with some of my grandfather's after-shaving talcum—I never used it, so I didn't have any of my own—but this only made me look worse: like a clown with piebald face make-up on, white jaws and forehead and a bright-hued nose sticking out between them. So I scrubbed it off again with a towel and finally, with my hat tipped down low over my face, went to see a doctor, more out of mental distress than bodily discomfort as yet.

He told me what it was, jaundice. All I recall now is a series of brief but excruciating pains in the region of the liver, immediately following anything I took into my stomach. They bent me over double sometimes while they lasted, but luckily they didn't last long at a time. At that resilient, vitality-crammed age, pain is easily borne and quickly thrown off again, and a moment later forgotten. I was allowed to eat nothing but milk-toast for awhile, but I was so hungry that even that tasted good.

He also suggested I stay away from classes for the time being, I don't know whether because of the illness itself or for appearances' sake, and I was only too glad to, rather than face the stares and snickers my entrance into any classroom would have been bound to bring on. The young aren't particularly merciful toward one another; tact only comes later in life.

My own case always reminded me of the story making the rounds at the time, whenever I heard it then or later. About the two men riding on the trolley car, one of whom kept staring relentlessly across the aisle at the other. Finally the one being stared at couldn't stand it any longer, and raising his head he turned and asked plaintively, "Mister, why do you keep staring at me so?" "Because," the other told him disapprovingly, "you're the ugliest man I ever saw. I never *saw* anyone as ugly as you in my whole life before!" "I can't help it," answered the first one meekly, lowering his head again. "I know you can't," scowled the other indignantly. "But you could stay home at least, couldn't you?"

So I stayed in the house from then on, for twenty-four hours a day each day, waiting for my pigmentation to tone down again. It was a new experience for me, and to help fill up the complete vacuum that was produced by it I did the only thing it was possible for me to do: I read. I read every book there was in the house.

Now my grandfather's house had been built almost on the nose of the turn of the century, and he had bought it before it was completed. He moved in as its first occupant, along with the young wife, still living then, whom he had married when she was fourteen, and the two teenage girls who later became my mother and aunt.[8] It had many charming features, which were soon to disappear from such houses—along with the houses themselves, as the mass production of multiple-apartment buildings took over more and more. I don't know whether they had been put in to order for him or not. But I do know it had fireplaces in most of the rooms, even the bedrooms, topped by mantels, and in several of them they were flanked by floor-to-ceiling pier-glasses. It had intricate chandeliers in the main rooms, of brass or of prismatic glass, originally used for gas but later transformed for electricity. It even had oval frescoes painted on a couple of the ceilings, portraying cherubs frolicking about with overflowing cornucopias of roses and streamers of ribbons against an azure sky. I mention all this only to make a point. It had many such touches, that its period and price range regarded as niceties and refinements. But books it did not have, not in any great quantity, still less of any great *quality*. The one thing that might have affected the entire course of my life differently, if it had had them, it did not have.

Don't ask me what the reason was. There were a few polished maplewood shelves about the mantel in one room (referred to rhetorically as "the library" until the inaccuracy of the designation became too obvious and it became just "the front room, downstairs"); these held the entire lot. I got the impression they had been accumulated at random, haphazardly, without any organized plan. In other words, from time to time at irregular intervals, some members of the family had come home with an impromptu-bought book, or else had been given one as a gift. Then once in the house, they stayed in. But very few others came along afterward to join them.

I don't think it was due to a lack of culture. There was more than a little of that in the family. My grandfather spoke four of the main European languages and was an ardent opera fan. There were glass cases full of rare and artistic curios about the house which he had brought back from his travels in such places as Mexico, Siam, China, Japan.[9] My own mother was an accomplished pianist, and had studied under Scharwenka, one of the well-known teachers of her day.[10] But there are certain types of culture which do not necessarily tend toward bookishness; they are gracious rather than studious.[11] I suppose that is the answer.

There were a couple of items from the war years in the heterogeneous little stockpile (such as Gerard's *My Four Years in Germany*), but they didn't interest me much.[12] The war [WWI] had been over nearly a decade by then, and recent history is always stale. It takes time for it to mellow and come around full circle again, into its truer perspective.

It was the fiction that I found the real insult to my intelligence. Perhaps its nature had been conditioned by the fact that there had been two growing girls in the family for a considerable part of the time; I don't know. Then again that may not be fair. I came to realize, or to believe, later on, that there had been q greater change in fictional literature of the minor variety, between 1907 and 1917 (to pick two dates at random) than there had been in the whole fifty or even one hundred years before then.[13] Classics are always classics, and beyond time. But it is this mediocre stuff I mean. The tempo of real life beyond the bounds of literature had quickened immeasurably, and items such as I was now dredging up no longer reflected it. Besides which they hadn't even been good in their own right in the first place.

I wish I could remember what some of them were now, but I can't. All I know is they were rotten. If I were to say one of them had been *The Garden of Allah*, or one *Elizabeth and her German Garden*, I might be telling a lie, and maligning two perfectly decent books, for all I know.[14]

They seemed to get successively worse too, as I went along. I don't know why. Maybe some intuitive sense of selectivity had made me save the worst for last. Or maybe my anticipation kept wearing thinner all the time. But as I threw the final one down, the pain wasn't' in my liver, it was in my literary sensibilities (such as they were).

I remember writhing distressedly in the chair I'd spent so many sterile hours in, the past week or more. *"Any*body could write a better book than that!" I asserted to myself, through gritted teeth. *"Anybody!"* And then the next sequential was, "I bet even somebody who's not a writer could." And then the next, "I bet even I could, myself." And then in ultimate derogation, "With one hand tied behind my back!"

I got up and went looking through the house. I was alone in it at the time; I seemed to be alone in it pretty much of the time those days, except in the evenings. I collected a sheaf of loose yellow paper; it was all I could find, except some folded note-size stationery, which would have been too cramped. I opened my bureau drawer and extracted the cardboard laundry-wedge from one of my clean shirts, to give the paper something to rest up against. A pencil I had in my own right. And that was all you needed, it appeared, to write a book. That, and a little thing inside that ticked like a watch, called mind.

I went back to my chair and I cocked up one knee in front of me and touched the pencil-tip to my tongue.

In a little while I wrote a line. And my life's work had begun.

It was not only a line without a plot, it was a line without a chapter, and a line without even a paragraph. Just a detached line, completely out of context.[15]

Then I got a second one, to link up with the first. Then they started to pick up pace, until they were coming almost faster than my hand could handle them. Right there, on the spur of the moment, I devised and brought into play the series of shortcut symbols I used the rest of my life in writing material, until it had become so standardized with me it even crept over into my personal correspondence. Two crossed lines with a slantwise connection for "and"; a small *g* with a line under it for the ending "ing" on any word; the letter *y* for "you" and all its derivatives, "yours," "yourself," etc; the numeral *1* followed by "ce" for "once," similarly for "twice," and so on; "bec" for "because"; and many more. It seems cumbersome at first sight, but it became a great time-saver.

The stream of words was like an electric arc leaping across the intervening space from pole to opposite pole, from me to paper, later on from me to machine. It was tiring and it wouldn't let go, it seemed to ground you (if that's the word). *You* couldn't stop it, it had to stop by itself. Then it fizzled out again at last, as unpredictably as it had begun. It left me feeling spent for a little while after, and the octagonal yellow-enamel finish of the pencil was actually hot to the touch, not from the hold of my hand, but from the uninterrupted, slashing friction.[16]

I couldn't tell what it was, I still can't. Some kind of energy, I know, but that's all I know about it.

I've had it happen in the damnedest places, as inconvenient as— as the high-spot of love—when you're *not* making love and are not in a position to. Then again when I've had everything set for it, it wouldn't come on. Once after days of exploratory bicycling, I found a deserted little cove along the coastline south of Biarritz that seemed to be just what I was looking for for the rest of that summer.[17] I cycled down to it the next day with all my equipment, everything I needed, a shade for my eyes, *Gitanes*,[18] a couple bottles of French beer (but always for *after*, never before). It was an ideal place for it; not a person in sight, not even a house, for miles around, the relaxing sand, the blue Biscay water, the warm, soothing breeze blowing from it. Nothing happened, not a word would come; I finally dozed off. It was *too* quiet, not enough background sound; it was like writing in a vacuum.

On the other hand, it hit me with such violent immediacy one night when I was coming home in a taxicab, that I didn't even have time to pay him off, hop out and get inside; I was afraid I'd choke it off or stillbirth it if I didn't give it its head immediately. So I kept him standing there at the door with his meter going while I scribbled away furiously on the back seat under the dim roof-light, using every scrap of paper I could fish out of my pockets. It turned what would have been a mere seventy-five-cent haul into about two-dollars-and-eighty-five cents worth of taxi-ride, but it was worth every nickel. And nickels were like half dollars to me in those days.

I remember he said to me, not very perceptively, when I finally opened the door to step out, "You're a writer, hunh, that what you are?"

Yes, I was a writer, hunh, that's what I was.

It was a strange experience, though, that first day, making up things on paper as you went along. But by the second day a lot of the strangeness had already worn off, I was beginning to feel at home doing it. Once or twice in the beginning, too, I'd stop short and read over what I'd done so far, and be tempted to crumple the paper into a ball and throw it away, thinking: "What am I doing this for? This is childish. What am I wasting my time like this for?" Then that stopped too. By the time I had about three or four of the yellow sheets covered on both sides (frugally) with my close-spaced handwriting, my innate sense of thrift came to the rescue. It already seemed too valuable to throw away. Not intrinsically so much as by reason of the amount of time and effort I'd put into it. I wanted something back for that.

I never threw away much that I'd written, later on. Even when I had to take out just a single line or even phrase from one story, because a rewrite job demanded it or it had become otherwise inappropriate, if I liked it well enough I didn't just cross it off, I tore off the paper it rested on in a whole, thin, page-wide strip, and pinned or clipped that aside somewhere for future use in some other story yet to come. Then when the proper niche for it finally came along, I put it back in.[19] I've always been a peculiarly thrifty writer, for some obscure reason. Maybe I had a subconscious fear that my supply of word-ideas might run out, and I better not waste any of them. But I think a more accurate explanation would be that I valued my own word-work so highly, I hated to discard any of it. Which is as it should be. A writer who doesn't believe in himself to the hilt can never be much of a writer.

I think now it was a bad thing, from the short-range point of view, to have saved it [*Cover Charge* (1926)], but a necessary thing in the long run, to ensure my future as a writer. It wasn't worth saving in itself, but if I hadn't saved it, I probably never would have written another. I would have remembered the fiasco of the first time, and there wouldn't have been enough encouragement to warrant my giving up an equal amount of time and effort a second time. In other words, though it did me no credit, was just an exercise rather than a finished product, I'm pretty sure I wouldn't have gone on to become a writer without it. To which the natural corollary immediately arises: Well, would that have been a loss? Who needed you? True, but everyone has to do something, everyone has to do the best he can. He's allowed that much, at least.

I started out with one line, as I said. Well, any writer does, any story or any book does. Then the line became a paragraph, the paragraph a page, the page a whole scene, the scene a whole chapter. But this stood alone, by itself, in the middle of nowhere. A scene without a story to go with it, in other words.[20]

I wrote out from it in both directions, forward toward the ending and backward toward the beginning. Finally, I'd stretched it out forward as far as I could, and stretched it out backward as far as I could, and the thing was suddenly over, finished.

"So that's how you write a book!" I marveled, hardly able to believe it myself.

But the whole thing was still formless anyway; it had no plot progression, no dramatic unity, no structural discipline. There was a great deal of such writing being done at the time, it was called "slice-of-life," I think, and it deliberately avoided plot and structure. But the big difference between it and my own effort was this: these others had something to write about, at least. I didn't. They knew something about life, even if it was only one small segment, one infinitesimal microcosm of it, and they were writing about the part they knew. I knew nothing about any part of it, so therefore I was writing about something I knew nothing about.

What I was actually doing was, not writing autobiographically, which every beginner does and should, but writing objectively, which should come along only a good deal later. What saved it from being any worse than it was, was a facility with words, which probably had been latent in me all along.

But I came to realize later, as I grew a little, that it was far better to be short on words, scantily supplied, poor in them, so long as you could sprinkle the few you had over a damn good basic situation (which could carry you along by itself, almost without words), than to be able to work them into a rich weave, make them glitter, make them dance, range them into vivid descriptions and word pictures, and in the end have them covering nothing but a great big hole.[21]

In one of my earlier clinkers, not the first but one that came soon afterward, on trying to reread it a few years later, I found out with the help of two spaced pencil marks that it had taken me a full one-and-a-half pages (and compact print and not unduly wide margins either) to describe a man riding up in an elevator from the ground floor to the third.[22] Nothing happened that might have extenuated it; there was no knife fight, no pickpocket observed plying his trade. No one else was on the elevator with him. He just stood there and thought.

It could have been done in one four-part line that barely stretched all the way across the page, like this: "He got in, the car started; the car stopped at the third and he got out again."

But I know what the matter was. I knew I had nothing to say, I knew I had to fill out two-hundred-odd pages to get it up to minimum book length, I was afraid I'd never make it, so I dragged out everything to unutterable length, just to fill all that empty white space with little black marks, no matter what the marks were or what they said. If I'd cut the thing down to appropriate size, I'd have had a medium-length short story there, but even that would have had the same defect: it would have been all about nothing at all. The real solution would have been not to let the damn thing be published at all, that would have been the best cure for it. But asking a young beginning author to deny himself publication is like asking a thirsty tongue-dangling pup to deny himself a drink of water.

I am dwelling on this first writing copy of mine at such great and unwarranted length, because I want to explain the defects inherent in it, and how I learned only later that they were defects and that I must try to avoid them. If there is one thing that is sure death to a writer it is, not having too hard a time of it, having too easy a time of it. That can stunt him, abort him, cripple him ineradicably. If he can get published without having to exercise self-discipline in his turn-out, he may never really learn how to write well at all. I was lucky, I got a second chance. I finally learned to do my job competently only in the mid-Thirties, after I'd already been hitting print steadily for eight years.[23] It would have been a lot better if everything I'd done until then had been written in invisible ink and the reagent had been thrown away. If you can't write a thing well, don't write it at all; leave it unwritten, for somebody else to write. The world doesn't need stories that badly, it has too many already.

(I am also particularizing so on this first piece of crap I turned out in order to get all such occupational references over with and out of the way once and for all before going ahead. For the rest of this account, just: I wrote, and that's all. No titles, no details, no anything.)

About halfway through the preliminary stage (pencil manuscript on yellow paper) my color, after stubbornly refusing to budge an inch for a long time, suddenly began tapering off again as rapidly, in reverse, as it had first turned yellow. In about two days I was completely white-skinned again—a little *too* white at first, but at least white. I was starved and gaunt, but well again. I went right back to classes without waiting for a complete recovery. I had to, because there was a lot of work to catch up on. But the first couple of days I was so weak I practically toppled over sidewise into my seat in each classroom I went into, instead of seating myself the usual way, bottom down. And of course I had to cut out writing in the daytime.

But it had become such a fixed habit by now, such a part of my daily routine, I was so hooked on it, that I couldn't have given it up for love nor money. So every evening after my meal was over I'd sit there, anywhere from nine to eleven-thirty or twelve, in the room on the second floor that had the grand piano in it, with the white cicatrices on its lid where spilled gin from my pocket flask had eaten into the ebony patina, the door closed, the family out or inaudible, a single lamp lit behind me on a pedestal in the corner, the one I called the elephant lamp because it had come from Burma or somewhere and had an elephant's head, complete with tusks and trunk, on each side of its base; bending over my knee scribbling away, with that frayed piece of cardboard (or some lineal successor) for a surface. Every now and again I'd take a breather, lean back, to rest my back and ease my neck, and put out even the one light, to facilitate the gathering of new thoughts for the pencil-bout to come.

I never forgot those chiaroscuro seances in that second-floor room. Lights up, writing; lights out, getting ready to write some more; lights up, at it again. I like that kid, as I look back at him; it's almost impossible not to like all young things anyway, pups and colts and cubs of all breeds. But I feel dreadfully sorry for him, and above all, I wish and pray, how I wish and how I pray, that he had not been I. He might have had a better destiny, if he hadn't been, he might at least have had a chance to find his happiness.

Sometime in the latter part of that spring the blamed thing finally came to an end, simply, as I have said before, because both ends had been stretched out as far as they would go from an arbitrary mid-point, not necessarily the mid-point of the story, but the point at which I had begun doing it.

I felt at a loss at first. I'd lived with it so long, been doing it so long, that there was a gap there where it had been. This was the one main reason which decided me to type it up. It gave me an excuse to stay with it longer, keep on "doing" it, even though now I wasn't really writing it any more, I was just changing its format. A second and probably even more valid one was that it was practically unreadable to anyone but myself in its present form. I'd not only written on the undersides of the yellow sheets, I'd written many of them upside-down. Some undersides belonged to the topsides of other sheets altogether and not the ones they were physically attached to. Afterthoughts, which sometimes came two or even three pages later, were marked off by matching stars or asterisks, one at the place where they were, the second to show where they were supposed to be. And then finally, I had this abbreviatory or semi-shorthand system of my own. The thing needed a Rosetta stone or more likely a compass for you to be able to follow it through with any degree of ease.

But the one motive that did *not*—I repeat and underline—did *not* enter into my going through the laborious chore of setting it up in typescript, was the idea of showing it somewhere with a view toward publication, or of showing it anywhere at all for any reason whatever. It wasn't that I didn't have confidence in it. I did. It had been done by me, so my young ego had overweening confidence in it. But I didn't have confidence that others would have confidence in it. Which wasn't quite the same thing at all.

So I decided it had to be typed. And to do this there had to be a typewriter.

Yet I didn't have the money to get myself one. I might have managed to squeeze enough together, over a laborious period, if I had been able to let it accumulate. But I never could seem to do this. In the first place acquiring a typewriter had never been a long-term aim of mine, something to try to save up for. I only felt the need for one as and when I came to the end of the novel. Until then I'd never thought about owning one. And secondly, there was always something more immediate, transitory but more immediate, to drain away the scanty little money that was all I was ever able to round up at one time.

I had become a very frivolous-minded young character by this time. Anything superficial and topical that came along attracted me, and I had to have it. And the Twenties were full of bonfire-like fads that blazed up across the country and then died down again almost as swiftly. Whether it was a pair of "Oxford bags," voluminous trousers that made the wearer's legs appear to have the girth of an elephant's; or a yellow rain slicker with slangy, supposedly dashing, inked mottoes self-inscribed on the back, implicitly aimed at the eyes of passing girls; or one of those sweaters, typical of the Twenties, with a mosaic of multicolored diamonds across the front—I had them all, and there was never any money left to put aside toward a typewriter. Every few weeks I gladly skipped lunch for a couple of days in a row just to be able to buy the latest record by Red Nichols or George Olsen.[25] (I had a stack of them that climbed halfway up one wall of the room like a serrated, shellacked chimney-stack, always threatening to topple, somehow always staying up.) And at that, they only cost eighty-five cents apiece in those days, which will give you an idea of how hard up I was most of the time.

Admittedly, most youngsters, boys and girls alike, as the teens verge toward the twenties,[26] do have pretty much that same frivolous, frolic-bent outlook. It's a part of growing up, I guess. But in me the change-over had been too sudden and too drastic to be explained by that alone. I hadn't had any of that in me before, not even the germ of it; all through the latter part of my childhood and the early part of my teens I'd been a notably serious-minded, reserved, pensive sort of boy, seldom smiling, seldom laughing; with every earmark of being intended to turn into a grave, dignified, intellectual sort of man (probably along with the concomitant of taking myself too seriously). And then this sudden switch took place.

I have often wondered, since, if the episode with Vera didn't have something to do with it.[27] Only after that did the change seem to come about. But knowing Vera may only have accelerated what was bound to come anyway. The path you follow is the path you have to follow; there are no digressions permitted you, even though you think there are.

I know now, even if I didn't then, that I didn't actually want those trivialities for their own sakes, what they were in themselves. They were symbols, necessary to my new outlook, which finally became my only outlook, to my new viewpoint, my new philosophy of life (it's perfectly valid to call it that, for no matter how young I was, I certainly had a life, and therefore was to be allowed a philosophy to go with it).

For instance, although I already smoked heavily and incessantly, and continued to do so for the entire rest of my life, I never once took a moment off to recognize that I actually didn't like the taste of cigarettes. Similarly, I was already beginning to drink sporadically (not habitually, of course; how could I have, yet?), but with such diligence when I did do it that on at least two occasions I fell flat on my face on the sidewalk and lay there unable to get up again. The first time, a group of good samaritans, youths a few years older than myself, half-carried me back to my own door, legs dragging along behind me; how I got home the second time I no longer recall, but I apparently made it unharmed. The streets of New York were a lot safer during the late hours at that time than they became later on, and I never had much in the way of money on me anyway.

But neither during this apprentice stage nor, far more pertinently, during the cascades that I let pour over me in a distant after-time, did I ever stop and think, stop and notice, that I actually didn't like the taste of liquor. I didn't; it always took the second drink to kill the unattractive taste of the first. And the last drink of all still didn't taste any better than the first had. It was just that by then liquor didn't have any taste at all.

It was as though I were either trying to cover up *from* something, or cover *up* something, or both.[28]

It is a wrong thing and a bad thing to pervert yourself like this. There is nothing more wrong, more bad, that you can do. You don't harm others, only yourself. You destroy the you that was meant to be, that was placed there to be, that would have been and should have been, far more thoroughly than the world around you ever could have. This is a form of suicide-in-life, and I committed it.[29]

I would have been a great writer. I would have been a great and a good man. I would have left a name that would have gone down in the annals. And, speak it low, I would have led a happy life.

This credo of escape from responsibility, of fun and of the unserious, was in the atmosphere, the climate of the times, it's true; a whole generation, more or less, shared it; but in others it waned and dwindled and finally expired as the period that had produced it passed away. (The Depression came, and then their children came, and they were too careworn by then to ever go back to it anymore.)

But in me it never did. It became locked into my heart and mind so that I could never get it out again. Suppressed for long periods at a time, first because of a complete lack of money, and then later because my instinct warned me that it could be toxic to my work if not held down, still it was always there, latent there, not to be denied; it accompanied me through the money-staved Thirties, the stirring war-years, the bated, fear-ridden Fifties, undiminished even into the Sixties. It was the perfect counterpoint to the sense of personal, private doom that had been in me all my life, ever since one night when I was eleven and, huddling over my own knees, looked up at the low-hanging stars of the Valley of Anahuac, and knew I would surely die finally, or something worse.[30] I had that trapped feeling, like some sort of a poor insect that you've put inside a downturned glass, and it tries to climb up the sides, and it can't, and it can't, and it can't.

I was a true son of the Twenties, carrying them with me through the long after-years. I made the Twenties last for forty years. This was the only possible answer, the only answer there could be: after me, the downpour....

I needed a typewriter.

Now Ken comes into it; Ken had one.[31]

Ken was a year ahead of me in school, a senior, and just a few years ahead in age, not too many. But at that particular point in my life the spread between us was as great as ten or fifteen years would have been later on. Ken had lived, and I hadn't begun to yet. He'd been in the 1918 war and had come out of it with something the matter with his leg. He had to spare it slightly, and he used a cane when he walked, which gave him a gallant-young-soldier aspect that was apparently anything but a handicap as far as girls were concerned. His nerves hadn't fully knitted together again yet, either; I know this was no pose, because I was walking along beside him one day when a kid exploded a firecracker out in the middle of the street with the sharpness of a whip-crack, and Ken gave a heist almost out of his shoes that couldn't possibly have been faked, and turned around and cursed the kid bitterly for the shock that he'd given him.

He had that cynical, disillusioned outlook which was widespread among his whole generation, the young men who had come out of the war, and in his particular case at least, I think he was fully entitled to it. Pre-1918 America, for a great nation, had been unbelievably provincial and nineteenth century, and a lot of these boys had been turned inside out emotionally, even without any physical injury.[32]

But in Ken's protective shield of disbelief and rejection (if that's what it was), there was one loophole allowed, one exception made. That was myself. I'm not too sure how this came about. Youth is idealistic, no matter how hard it tries not to be, and Ken was certainly not old yet. I was sounding off at great length one night soon after we first met, a thing which came easy to me when I had a listener who had my confidence, and I happened to describe how clean and sparklingly fresh and brand new the world always seemed to me when I first opened my eyes each morning, and how I was sure each time that it was going to turn out to be a wonderful day ahead and something wonderful was going to happen, and even if it didn't, then it surely would the next day; in other words, just being alive was great.

He looked at me and said, quietly but earnestly, "You restore my faith in the world."

With this as its inception, he developed a sort of protective, older-brother attitude toward me. He even carried this so far as to sponsor my initiation into the knowing of women, in the scriptural sense, pretty much on the same principle as in certain primitive tribes where, I understand, the striplings had to face up to certain tests and ordeals before they were allowed to claim full manhood. Ken's motive, I surmise, was a belief that it was far more preferable from a hygienic, or shall I say antiseptic, standpoint that this take place under his carefully regulated supervision than that I be allowed to roam around at will like a stray pup.

However, he didn't discuss that part of it with me at all. There was no suggestiveness nor even flippancy in the way he went about it; on the contrary, he carried it out with a grave, conscientious air of responsibility, almost like a confirmation or a first communion, no irreverence intended. He got me lubricated with gin first, up to a carefully determined, but not excessive, point. Then he called up and arranged a double date or rendezvous for four with two girls in a far-upper West Side apartment, one of whom he already knew. (I think it was in the Washington Heights section, but I was never able to locate it again afterwards.)

I have a recollection of a completely blacked out living room, the four of us unseen in the dark, with an occasional faint stirring or whispering, and once in awhile a sudden laugh. And above all, of a record that never stopped playing the whole time from first to last: "I'm Just Wild About Harry." Each time the needle got to the end and started that empty, rustling sound, a pair of stockinged feet would pad across the carpet in the dark—Ken's girl, for she was the hostess—and she'd switch the needle arm back to the beginning and start it over again. I don't know why she never turned it over on the flip side, but she never did. Maybe she already knew what was on the other side, and didn't like it. Or maybe she just wanted to get back to Ken in a hurry, and it took too long to lift it off, turn it around, and put it back on again in the dark.[33]

I never again could hear that piece without remembering that pitch-black room, though everything else is gone now, the girls' names, their very faces, and even Ken himself.

After that once, I was on my own. I'd been inducted. I often wondered if his own first experience had been less than happy, and if that was why he took such an altruistic interest in mine. I never asked him. But mainly his attitude lifted it above what it might otherwise have been, and made it a commendable act of guidance instead of just a rather sordid partnership. He cleaned it up. I'm not being facetious here. It was done in an honest, manly, fraternal way, and all the smut taken away from it. It was something to look back on appreciatively for the spirit in which it was rendered, and I always have. He was nice to know and a good friend to have straight down the line.

That was Ken, for you.

He was from Iowa, and like me he didn't live on campus. But in his case, not having any family in New York to stop with as I did, he lived in a furnished room just on the edge of it. The house was run by a Mrs. Collins, a fragile wren-like little woman, who was fond of mothering him, he used to tell me. What this consisted of I'm not sure; I suppose the usual tidying up on his mornings after, which incidentally he needed a great deal. I can still see her now, with her gray-white hair drawn back and knotted tightly just over the top of her head, always in a faded blue work dress with an apron over it.

Anyway, I'd been in the room hundreds of times with him, and he had a typewriter in it. I asked him if I could come in and use it to do some work.

"Sure," he said. And then he asked, not unnaturally, "What kind of work, class-work?"

"No," I mumbled evasively.

One partly warded-off question led to another—this unfortunate block or impediment of mine, being unable to tell an outright direct lie, was a distinct handicap when trying to keep anything covered up—until finally, by overriding a succession of defensive no's, he wormed it out of me. "I'm trying to write a book," I said deprecatingly, averting my face slightly. At least, to my credit, I wasn't cocksure enough to say "I am writing," just "trying to write." I recall that much.

I saw a quizzical glint in his eyes for a moment. I don't know what it was; half amused, as by a precocious small boy, half amazed, as by an everyday colleague with unsuspectedly far-reaching ambitions. That was the best I could read in it, anyway. It didn't last long enough to be too flagrant, in any case.

I don't know why I had such innate reticence about it, almost an embarrassment or jolt to one's delicacy, like being caught in public with your pants down. I felt even more strongly about it with my family than I did with Ken, for he was years nearer my age bracket, and I was more outspoken with him, as one always is to a friend. I'm sure my family would have gladly staked me to a typewriter, if they'd had any idea what I wanted it for, but I couldn't bring myself to tell them. From first to last they remained completely unaware of what I was doing, the whole time I was writing the book.

I was still this way years after, at least as far as family was concerned. To the end of her life, my mother never read a single line I wrote. Not because she didn't want to, but because I prevailed upon her not to. She often asked me to let her see something. "Not this," I'd say each time. "Wait'll something better comes along." And take it out of her hands and close it. I wanted to make a good showing, I guess; I wanted her to read only the best. The next one was always going to be better than this one. Then when the next came along, the one after was going to be better than that. She was docile and trusting in everything that concerned me. Perfection never came along. She never read a word I wrote.[34]

Ken had Mrs. Collins give him a second key and he turned it over to me. I showed up there around nine with all my paraphernalia, a cardboard box crammed with closely scribbled yellow sheets, a wad of blank white typing paper (I was tactful enough to supply that, at least), cigarettes galore, but no allowance for nor thought of a carbon- or emergency second-copy, let myself in, took off my coat and tie, and went to work. He was out, of course.

It went very well the first night or so. Slow but well. Two fingers, but a labor of love. A lot of close peering, a lot of back strain, a lot of smoking of costly Lucky Strikes (to me they were, anyway: fifteen cents a pack), but a lot of contentment. Then about the third, maybe the fourth night, after I'd been there about an hour, the door was suddenly keyed open and Ken showed up with a young lady companion.

Impersonal hellos were said all around without any names being given, and I reluctantly lowered my poised paws. He gave me a look which I understood, and I gave him one back to show I understood. I painstakingly gathered up all my written material, even the sheet currently in the roller. I didn't want her to pick it up afterward, during one of their breathing spells, and read it aloud and maybe laugh over it with him. Impersonal so-longs were said all around, and I tractably took my leave.

I don't think, actually, looking back now, that the amorous side of Ken's life, or whatever you want to call it, was either more extensive or frequent than that of any other young buck his age and in similar circumstances. I think it simply seemed so, exaggeratedly so, because it impinged on my own interests. Every rendezvous meant an eviction.[35] I liked him very much then and I love him very dearly now; he may be gone by now, but even if he is, I still wouldn't want to credit him posthumously with a greater prolificness than he deserves to be charged with. These things should be weighed carefully before they are spoken. What is a compliment in youth may not be one in age, and may be a derogation in death, for all I know. It probably was the spaced, unremitting steadiness of it rather than its numerical rate of occurrence that threw me.

I don't know what the exact ratio was, but I would guess that out of fifteen potential work nights, I lost six. This wouldn't have been so bad if the six had occurred in succession. Then I would have still had nine clear nights all to myself. But they didn't, he would have had to be superhuman for that; besides, he wasn't consciously taking me into his considerations, he wasn't consciously considering at all, it just happened when it happened. (One night I heard him give a sudden, subdued exclamation as he arrived outside the door with someone, as if he'd only just then remembered that I was inside.) Every time an interruption happened, it took me a couple of nights to warm up again, get back in the swing again, even in a case like this, which was merely transcription, not composition. I've always been that way about my work. Then each time, just as I got my rhythm going, he seemed to get his going, and he'd walk in on me again.

What might have been expected to happen, finally did happen. One night through a fluke of timing, I got there after he was already in the room. The door was fastened on the inside, wouldn't open to my key. Instead of taking it for granted and going off again, I knocked to make sure; I guess I hated the thought of another wasted evening.

After a very considerable delay, and two or three more knocking, the door opened very narrowly and reluctantly, a mere few inches, and he stuck a segment of his face through. It looked all puffy and yeasty, as though he'd been asleep.

"I've got somebody in here with me," he said in a drowsy voice. "Can you make it some other time?"

"When don't you have?" I groused (rather arrogantly, now that I think of it). "You always have. When am I going to get this blamed thing through?"

Close friends or not, we weren't any too well pleased with one another at the moment, if I recall the looks we exchanged.

With that, he closed the door abruptly in my face. I thought it was in curt dismissal, and turned and walked sullenly back toward the street entrance. (His room was the first door on the right as you entered on the ground floor. Logistics must have played a part in his selection of it.) Just as I reached the street threshold, he reopened his door and hissed surreptitiously at me to come back. I turned and went back. Whereupon he opened the door a little wider, but still none too generously, and thrust something out at me through it. I just had time to instinctively shove out my forearms, undersides up, to catch it, when he dumped the typewriter into them. It was a hefty thing, and my unprepared knees nearly buckled for a minute under the unexpected weight.

"Take it back to your place with you and work there," he muttered in a confidential undertone.

We looked at each other for a minute. Then a grin of satisfaction slowly spread over my face. He grinned back at me. The brief interlude of irritation was over. He closed the door. Then reopened it a third and called after me, in a more full-bodied voice than he'd used previously (I guess his guest had finally awakened, with all the stirrings and openings and closings that had been going on): "Be careful of it now, don't let anything happen to it. I'm going to need it to do my Master's on this summer."[36]

It weighed a ton. It was an Underwood, I think, a non-portable, about a 1912 model, with an overbearing, top-heavy upper carriage, but I managed to get it home, staggering bow-legged the whole way. I could have gotten a piano home unaided in those days if I'd wanted to badly enough.

I found the perfect thing to rest it on: the table part of what had once been a sewing machine, dating from the days of the household's glory, when the "girls" (mother and aunt) had had a professional dressmaker come in by day to work on their wardrobes. I found it at the back of a closet, and its small oblong surface fit the base of the machine nicely, with a strip of margin left over wide enough to take a pack of Luckies. The diminishing pile of yellow sheets, I kept on the seat of a chair turned sideward toward me.

I went to work, on the last leg of this long, irrational process that I was somehow caught up in. And now there were no more interruptions, at least not of the stature of Ken's biological essays.[37] There was a trifling distraction for a few nights, but I didn't allow it to become an interruption. I was working in a room at the back, and you could look into it on a diagonal from the bedroom window of the apartment alongside, which extended deeper than our house did. Two girls there started to peek in at me. I suppose it was the sound of the typewriter that had attracted them in the first place. I'd hear suppressed tittering and giggling, but when I turned my head around each time, the window would be empty, they'd pull their heads back. I finally glimpsed them: two sleek bobbed-haired heads, one jet black, the other pale blonde.

I knew what was making them laugh. I was working in my trousers and undershirt, for the sake of comfort, and my arms were thin as toothpicks at that time. For that matter, so was most of the rest of me. I knew, also, that they weren't trying to flirt, they were just at that giddy age when they liked to play games and attract attention to themselves. They were about fifteen, and I looked down on them condescendingly from the lofty height of my own superior age. I didn't bother lowering the shade, for that would have made the room stuffy, nor putting on my outer shirt, for that would have made me feel cramped. I just stopped turning my head around, and as I'd expected, in a little while the semi-precocious teasing died down of its own accord, for lack of response. Incidentally, some time later I met them both more formally, on the street, and they turned out to be very nice girls: Carolyn and Helen. We remained steadfast acquaintances for quite a few years after that, although they never did quite catch up to me in age.

I was sitting there one day working on page 22, and I was alone in the house at the time—I always seemed to be alone in the house—when the doorbell rang. I got up and went hustling down the stairs, giving those swift swings around the turns I always gave in those days. The front door had a glass upper half, with a translucent glass curtain over it, of fine mesh or net. As I came up to it, something told me that the outline I saw standing on the other side of it was that of a policeman, I guess because of the flat-topped headgear, the uniform cap, that I could dimly make out, soft-focused through the curtain. I opened the door, and it was.

We looked at each other, for just a second only.

He asked me if my name was, and gave my grandfather's name.

I told him no, but that that was my grandfather's name.

He gave it to me quick then, and bluntly. I guess he thought that was the best way to do it. Or maybe he didn't know any other way. I think it was the best way, probably. The quickest is the best.

"He's dead," he said. "He dropped dead suddenly in a friend's office downtown. He's down there now."[38]

"I'll get in touch with the rest of the family," I said indistinctly. I heard myself say it, but I don't know whether he did or not.

Then I looked at him and he looked at me, some more. It wasn't a pleasant job to have to do. It wasn't a pleasant thing to have done to you, either. I closed the door. I wouldn't have wanted to do it. But if I had had to do it, I think I would have put my hand on the other fellow's shoulder, even if only for a moment. I'm not saying anything against him. He did it just right. But everyone has his own way of doing a thing like that.

After everything was attended to and over, I went back upstairs and sat down where I'd been before, in front of the typewriter again. Not to write any more, but to think about it. It seemed the best place to be; I belonged there. It was the first time I'd ever come up against death. Face to face, I mean. Within that smaller replica of life itself, that living body, living entity: the family.

I didn't cry, I didn't know how. I hadn't cried since early childhood, and from then on I didn't cry again, except just once, and very briefly then. When I was down to my last nickel and sick of failing, a bartender happened to touch the exposed nerve of self-pity by handing me a free beer with the wrong kind of look on his face: too kind. I didn't cry again almost all the rest of my life through. I didn't cry even when my mother died, though my arm shook and my whole body too, with the wrench of realization, as I stood up with a brandy and toasted her, somewhere sight unseen.[39] But you don't have to cry to love someone, to miss them.

There had been a companionability between us that skipped not one generation but two. Sometimes there is. He used to like to have me go to the movies with him, I remember. We'd go on the average of, I don't know, about once a week, I guess. He didn't like to sit there alone, most likely. And it was a help to his walking to have someone along. He was beginning to suffer from hardening, and he had to stop every now and then to let the pain ease off. But still, when all that has been said, there was a preference there, a tie. He could have had others instead. He never did. It was only I he wanted to have go with him, no one else. (He went downtown alone, for example, to carry out whatever business he had to transact; he had a special taxi that he hired on a monthly basis, to stop by and pick him up each day and then bring him back again, and of course in this way no one else needed to go with him.)

And on my side, the same thing could be said for me. I admit, it was convenient and helpful to have someone else pay my admission fee for me, I'd be a liar if I said otherwise. But that wasn't the reason I went with him. I went because I wanted to, because I liked being with him. There was a closeness there, that strange affinity that can spring up more easily between extreme age and extreme youth, sometimes, than it can between less widely spread age-divergents.

And the best proof of it is that never once during the enforced stops that we had to make, which were always more numerous on the way back than on the way out, for he was more tired by then and there was no longer the impetus to arrive on time at the picture's beginning, never once, and I lift my head in unfaltering sincerity, did I ever chafe or shift my feet or show annoyance; not only not outwardly, where it could have been seen, but not inwardly either, where it couldn't. Which

I think is the important point. I was loyal to him in my mind. Nobody else can know this but me, but I do know it. I've been glad ever since that I was. It brings a tiny drop of added peace to me now.

I'd stand there beside him uncomplaining, unquestioning as a companionable pup, until he'd say "It's better now, let's go on again."

Not sense of duty nor respect nor anything merely filial like that; not pity either, but something far less one-sided and far less patronizing: he was mine.

Down below somewhere, I could hear the Irish cook sobbing into her apron. I could tell her apron must be up before her face because the sobs had a buried, clothed softness to them. She must have come back from shopping for the table. No table tonight. Her name was Julia, and she'd been in the house since 1913, when she first came over. He'd even let her have her wedding party in it; the family had cleared out so she could have the run of all the rooms for one whole evening.

I remembered how I used to scuttle around the corner and get his cigarettes for him sometimes when he asked me to. I used to like to do it, I don't know why. A token of his confidence, maybe. I can still remember the brand. They were Egyptian, Melachrino Number Two, cork-tipped. I remembered so many little things. But were they little? What are little, what are large?

There had always been an inscrutable sort of rapport between us, from the very time I was born. Or at least old enough to be aware of and to share it. The first grandson, then the only grandson.[40]

He took me to my first opera, when I was eight: *Butterfly*, done by a traveling French company in Mexico City.[41] It was given in that handsome Palace of Fine Arts, Diaz' Taj Mahal, that wasn't completed until many years afterward; its stage had a glass curtain that had been designed by Tiffany, they said.[42]

This one experience had a strange and lasting effect on me. It didn't do too much for me musically at the time. I came away still preferring "Row Row Row" and "That Skeleton Rag," which we had on the piano-rack back at the little flat at 6 Calle de Pomona.[43] But it did give me a sudden, sharp insight into color and drama, that came back to the surface again years later when I became a writer, and was a great help to me.

And, oddly—since opera is basically an unrealistic genre—it also sparked a fervent, almost fanatic chauvinism in me that lasted out the rest of my boyhood. When Pinkerton first came onstage in his white ducks, I didn't pay any attention to what he was singing; all I kept thinking, in a bated, gaping, ecstatic, trance-like state, was: "That's my country's uniform. He's wearing the uniform of my country." And my small chest swelled up with something as buoyant and as dizzying as helium gas. Patriotism. And just as liable to explosion, when it's carried in thousands of chests instead of just one, and they're grown ones and not a boy's.

Then again, at the beginning of the hara-kiri scene, when Cho-Cho-San parked the little baby Trouble in front of a screen, and stuck an American flag into his hand to wave, the same thing happened. I was caught up in this breathless, almost religious emotion, telling myself: "That's my country's flag. My country's flag."

And when a few members of the audience, which must have been predominantly Mexican, I suppose, equally chauvinistic but on the opposite side of the fence, let out some scattered, perfunctory hisses, I whirled around in my seat and climbed half up over the top of it, to glare and try to find them out. Until my grandfather, with a suppressed smile, had to touch me remindingly and say: "Watch the stage, sonny, watch the stage."

Oh, I had always known that I was American, of course. I had always known that I'd been born in New York; I could even vaguely recall a few scenes from it (they'd taken me away from it, the first time, when I was only three). But until this event, it had been more or less a quiescent factor, something taken for granted. Now suddenly it sharp-focused, came into full realization. A small boy in a foreign country. I walked home on air, my head high, my heart glowing, a secret dream, a secret pride, a secret fulfillment, all in one, now in me, that could never be taken away from me again. Endlessly, mystically, glorying in it: "I'm an American. I'm one of them. One of those."[44]

Strange is loneliness; it still longs to have something to belong to, some group, some aggregate.

I wandered down into his room and moved around it, looking at things, before going back upstairs and sitting before the typewriter again. It was a way of saying good-bye, I guess. The only way *I* had, anyway. I knew what they were then, knew them all by heart then, but I can't remember now what they were. Just the things someone has around the room he has lived in. I'd shared it with him for awhile at one time a few years before, I can no longer recall what the reason was; maybe they were painting mine. He used to get up and take an ice-cold shower the first thing every morning. Not a drop of warm water. He'd snort and he'd bounce around in there, and he'd love it. Then he'd come out with his skin looking as pink and lustrous as a salmon.

I can still remember the way he looked, and I always will. He used to remind me a good deal of photographs I'd seen of Mark Twain. Not in facial resemblance so much, but he had that same mane of white hair, worn pompadour. A full head of it, not a hair missing. It had turned white, completely all-over white, when he was twenty-one. And with it a mustache that was just as entirely black, nor a white hair in it. (It wasn't touched up, I know that for a fact; he would have scorned such a thing.)

That night the phone rang, and it was the "boys" at the poker club where he went to play once a week, asking what was keeping him and saying they were holding up the game for him. I don't know: to me that was the most poignant, wrenching, of obsequious, sadder than all the orations and all the rituals, because it was so little and so human. The "boys" at the poker club were holding up the game for him, and how much longer was he going to be?

I wonder what they did with his chair that night. Moved it back, or let it stand there empty ("None for me this time, dealer"), or did somebody else take it?

I don't know why I dwell at such length on him, at peace so long ago. I guess because I've always had that strong feeling for anything that belonged to me. And strangely enough, so little ever really did.

The next day I was back in front of the machine again. I finished Page 22 and pulled it off the roller, and put in a blank, and started 23.

I suppose that's my tribute to him: remembering the page I was on when his life stopped, down through all the long years after. But what is it makes a tribute anyway? Roses? Candles? Tears? Who equates it? Isn't that just as good a tribute as any, remembering the number of a page on some forgotten book?

Roses die, candles go out, tears dry. The memory of the number on the page outlasts them all.

Well, it was finally finished, and, weighing me down bow-legged once more, the typewriter went back to Ken. (The only time there ever was a ringer in my lifetime work-partnership with you.[45]) Now something came up which might have been expected, but which I hadn't nevertheless. I had thought the borrowing of the typewriter had no strings to it.

"Well, aren't you going to let me see it?" he said. "I'd like to see what it's like."

"What for?" I hedged. "So you can tell me how rotten it is?"

"Do *you* think it's rotten?" he came back at me.

It was a trick question and I walked right into it.

"Like fun I do," I blurted out heatedly before I had time to think. It's very hard at that age not to speak up for yourself, particularly among your friends and equals. It's natural and healthful, it's part of the competitive instinct. Modesty only comes later, and if you examine it closely, is basically less likable than conceit, even though it appears not to be. The one is alive, the other has a touch of the moribund.

That was exactly what he'd wanted me to say. "Then why not let me see it?" he said sleekly. He had me there.

Then when I still tried to find a way of getting out of it, "I let you borrow my typewriter," he pointed out. I should have known that was coming; it was unanswerable.

It went on like that for over a week, possibly even two. I kept procrastinating, he kept asking. Finally his reminders started to get briefer and cooler each time we ran into one another, and I knew that he was on the point of stopping them altogether and becoming offended. The last thing I wanted to do was alienate him; he was at the head of my list of friends right then. It seemed a poor way to return the favor he'd done me, anyway. So I finally brought it over to the room one day and put it down on the same table where I'd done the preliminary typing. I felt a little sheepish about the whole thing. On the order of the old simile about the mountain bringing forth a mouse, most likely.

He kept it one hell of a long time. This was partly my fault— at least as much as it was his. From the moment the physical work on it stopped, I progressively lost interest in it. If I asked him about it at all, I don't recall. But if I did, only desultorily, maybe once or twice. After that I stopped asking. There were other things in life, a great many of them. In fact it was crowded with them. Lively outer things, not static inner ones like this.

Finally I actually forgot it for a considerable stretch of time. This is literal. I know it to be a fact, because when it finally did come back to mind, it came with a shock of recollection, which shows that it hadn't been there at all until just then. "Hey! I wrote a novel, and it's still over there in Ken's room!" About like that.

Writing had apparently been a habit only, and when the habit had nothing more to feed on, it wore off. The end-results in themselves didn't seem to interest me. Poring over sheets of paper for hours at a time, for weeks, for months on end, had lost its charm for me. And I know now, if only by hindsight, that there was very little chance at the time that I would ever have written anything again. It was too laborious a *métier*. Besides, I had said everything I had to say the first time; what did I have left to say?

But what motivated me finally to look him up and more or less flatly insist on his giving it back to me was not literary self-esteem or concern for it as literary preventer at all, but something quite different. In mentioning my grandfather a little while ago, I spoke of this instinct I have always had for clinging to—cherishing—whoever, whatever, belonged to me; this sense of *my own-ness*. It was partly protective, partly possessive, and I guess there was just a dash of stubbornness in it too. It was good and it was not so good. It made me loyal almost to the point of blindness in friendship, and consequently a potentially easy mark. It made me tight and wary almost to the point of travesty in business dealings with strangers. I think it would have made an exceptionally good husband out of me, if I'd only given myself enough time to get broken in.[46] (But a second strong trait, a basic solitariness, came into conflict here, and won out.)

It showed up now in the relatively minor matter of this typescript, but it was the same trait. The script was mine, it belonged to me, I had worked on it, created it, and I wanted it back. I fully intended to discard it, or at the very least push it out of sight into a drawer, but *I* wanted to be the one to do so, not anyone else. I didn't want to leave it lying around at random. To stretch a point, there was a little of the feeling in it that a man has when he has committed himself a little too freely on paper to a woman and wants his letters back. It sounds strange I know, but there was just a touch of that in it.

For some reason, I've never forgotten the night before I finally accosted Ken about it. The first few years afterward I used to look back on that night and tell myself it was my last night of full and entire obscurity. Then later on, with a little more perspective behind me, I came to realize how presumptuous and preposterous this was, and knew better. No silver splash of limelight suddenly showered me, from one night to the next. For either all my nights, for all my life, have been obscure, or else they all alike have not been. I was in those nights, I was part of them, I watched what I did with them, knew what I did with them, they were not obscure to me. Therefore they were not obscure at all. They were simply the nights of my life, as unchanged after as before.

But this was just a kid's egotism, I guess, trying to think of himself as an overnight celebrity. And I wasn't altogether to blame, for quite a few older people who should have been wiser and should have known better did nothing to discourage the impression. In fact they were probably the ones who first gave me the idea.

I went to see a picture-show that night, and I can still remember what the show was called: *Shore Leave*, with Richard Barthelmess.[47] Then later I went to the Hotel Lucerne, on Seventy-ninth Street, with a girl I met quite haphazardly in the Times Square area. It was an out-and-out pick-up, in the baldest sense of the word. I'd never done that before in my life, and I don't think I ever did it again afterward either. At least, not with anyone I didn't know, no matter how superficially, beforehand. I didn't particularly want to do it very much, at that. It was just that I didn't know what else to do with myself, it got lonely standing around after the crowds started to thin out and go home, but the lights continued to blaze down on the empty, naked-looking sidewalks.

For some reason their very brightness made it seem even lonelier and more barren than it would if it had been only dimly lighted. The emptiness wouldn't have been so conspicuous, I suppose. I remember how little particles of brightness, like mica fused into the cement of the sidewalk, twinkled under the glare of the Paramount Theatre marquee. Then when the marquee went out, they continued to glisten in the comparative shade. Compared to the dazzle that had gone before. And a flicker of wind blew a stray leaf of newspaper along.[48]

I don't know what brought it about, this episode. But sex was not the main motivating factor; a need for companionship probably was.

I came out of there into that particularly ugly, gloomy pewter-color the very early daylight often assumes (that is, if your own mood reflects it that way), and went back to the house, and changed and washed and had a cup of coffee. And then went right out again to my first class of the day. There was no time to sleep, and I knew if I had tried to squeeze some in, I would only have overslept, and then probably felt even more tired than I did as it was.

I ran into Ken on one of the campus cross-walks later in the day, and I stopped him and asked him rather gruffly when I was going to get my book back. I was in a scowly sort of mood anyhow, probably due to lack of sleep the night before, and I made up my mind that this time I wasn't going to let him put me off any longer.

It came out, after some prodding on my part, that he'd shown it to a friend of his, some girl he knew, and she had it at the moment. He'd spoken about it to her, and she'd become interested and asked him to let her see it.

I didn't like the idea at all, and I let him know it. "I turned it over to *you* to read, not anyone else," I railed at him accusingly. "What are you trying to do, pass it around from hand to hand all over the campus, until you have everybody knowing my business and laughing at me? Why don't you start a circulating library with it?"

She didn't attend the campus, this girl, he said placatingly. But always with that hint of patronizing amusement somewhere at the back of it that used to drive me wild. She worked downtown, she had a job as a typist or secretary, or maybe she was on the switchboard, I can no longer recall, at a small publishing house in the Forties.[49]

He'd only been trying to do me a good turn, he went on earnestly. She was in the middle of a book-atmosphere, heard talk about them every day, and he'd thought she might be able to give me a few helpful pointers about mine.

"Suppose it's lost, is that a good turn?" I challenged.

"I'll call up for you right now and show you it's not lost," he said soothingly.

We adjourned to the nearest dorm. He went into the public phone booth and closed it after him, while I paced back and forth on the lobby floor outside, head intently lowered, hands stretching my pockets out wide, tracing the line of the edge of the carpet with my feet in a childish sort of absorption, or even form of self-mesmerism. Much in the way that children, walking along a cross-lined sidewalk sometimes, will skip certain squares and put their feet only in others, making a pattern.

Everything he did irked me, and I felt he should do it otherwise and not the way he did do it. He should have been sober and brief and to the point, I felt. Instead he seemed (judging by his face) to make a light bantering chat out of it, and smiled a lot, and prolonged it interminably. I'd look up in warning reminder that I was waiting, and then look down again at my metaphysical coursing, but he went right on. Once he looked straight at me, or seemed to, with an outright grin on his face. I shot him a stern look back, but it glanced off his unfocused face like thistledown.

Finally the light went off and he came out and sat down on one of the beaten, leather-covered settees there, and looked up at me. I remained standing before him at first, in an attitude meant to indicate stricture. Whether he took it that way or not, I don't know. Later he was the one on his feet and I was doing the sitting as I received the news that it'd sold.[50]

II
The Poor Girl

In this chapter, Woolrich tells the tragic story of his "first-time love" with Vera Gaffney, an Irish working-class girl. Like a modern Cinderella, Vera laments having nothing suitable to wear as Woolrich's escort to a fancy birthday party. Managing a fleeting escape from poverty in a new dress and fur, Vera becomes the talk of the ball. Unlike Cinderella, however, Vera ruins her own chance to find true love and happiness.

This is a powerful tale, whose poetic narrative is characterized by subtle alternations in mood, fully developed portraits and an ironic melancholia. The chapter's themes are easily identified with Woolrich's mature noir fiction. Nearly twenty years later, for example, a succinct retelling of this tragic romance is whispered by Ladd Mason in the eighth chapter of The Black Angel *(1943). And the first published version of this love affair appears in Woolrich's very first novel,* Cover Charge *(1926). In that version of the story, a poor Irish girl named Vera gradually develops a cynical view of romance, culminating in her aggressive "love-bite" upon meeting the leading male character at a block party.*

Oddly, this episode takes place in 1922-1923, and therefore predates Woolrich's bout with jaundice, described in Chapter 1. (Yet the original typescript clearly indicates that "The Poor Girl" should be "STORY #2" of Blues of a Lifetime.*)*

Everyone has a first-time love, and remembers it afterward, always, forever. I had a first-time love too, and I remember mine:

There was a fellow named Frank Van Craig, a year or possibly two years older than I, who lived a few doors up the street from me.[1] I called him Frankie, as might be expected at that time of our lives, and we were more or less inseparable, although we had only got to know each other a fairly short while before this.

His father was a retired detective of police, who lived on his pension, and the mother had died some years before, leaving this forlorn little masculine menage of three (there was a younger brother, still of school age) to get along as best they could. Frankie used to speak of his father patronizingly as "the old man." But gruff and taciturn as the father was, embittered by his loss and withdrawn into his shell, there must have been some deep-felt if unspoken bond between the two of them, for more than once, when I'd stop by for Frankie, I used to see him kiss his father respectfully and filially on the forehead before leaving. It touched me oddly, and I used to think about it afterward each time I saw it happen, for I had no father, and even if I had had, I couldn't visualize myself kissing him like that; it didn't seem right between two men.[2] But Frankie was my friend, and I was too loyal to entertain even a secret disapproval of him.

Frankie had a job in a machine- or tool-shop, but that was merely his way of earning a living. His real avocation was amateur boxing. He spent every spare moment at it that he could: evenings after his job, Saturdays, holidays. And he was good. I used to go down with him sometimes to the gym where he trained and watch him work out: spar with partners, punch the bag, chin the parallel bars, skip rope and all the rest. Then when we'd come away afterward, I used to walk along beside him with a feeling almost akin to adulation, proud to have him for a friend.

It was this feeling that had first brought us together, in what amounted on my part, at least in the beginning, to a mild but unmistakable case of hero-worship. He had the athletic prowess and the rough-and-readiness of disposition that I would have given anything to have had myself, and that I could tell was going to be lacking in me for the rest of my life; otherwise, it would already have appeared by this time. Then when this preliminary phase blew over as I became habituated to him, we became fast friends on a more evenly reciprocal basis, for there were things about me that I could sense he, in his turn, looked up to and wished he had.

At any rate, we were strolling along Eighth Avenue one evening side by side, under the lattice-work of the El,[3] when a very pretty girl of about my age, who was coming from the opposite direction, gave him a smile of recognition, stopped beside us and said hello to him. She was blonde, with a fair, milk-and-roses Irish complexion and hazel eyes lively as spinning pinwheels. Her pale hair was smooth and cut evenly all around at ear-tip level, with just a clean, fresh-looking part running up one side of it to break the monotony of its evenness.

After a few words had been exchanged, he introduced us with a characteristically gruff amiability. "Con meet Vera," he said. "Vera, meet Con." But our eyes had already become very well acquainted by this time.

"Hello Con," she said, and smiled.

"Hello Vera," I said, and smiled back.

Now that I'd met her I remember becoming more diffident than before I'd met her, and having less to say. (I'd already been talking to her before the introduction.) But she didn't seem to notice, and he on his part, obviously unattached, showed no constraint.

We stood and chatted for a while and then we parted and went our ways, on a note of laughter at something that he'd said at the end.

But I looked back toward her several times, and once, I saw her do it too, and somehow I knew it was meant for me and not for him.

"You know her well?" was the first thing I asked him.

"She lives around here," he answered indifferently, implying, I think, that she was too familiar a part of his surroundings to be of any great interest to him.

Then he turned around and pointed out the house. "Right over there. That one on the corner. See it?"

It was a six-story, old-law, tenement building, one of an almost unbroken line that stretched along both sides of Eighth, from the top of the park well up into the Hundred-and-Forties. Its top-floor windows were flush with the quadruple trackbeds of the Elevated, two for locals, two for expresses—two for downtown, two for up.

"She lives on the top floor," he went on. "I been up there. I went up and met her family once, when I first started to know her. Her family are nice 'nd friendly."

"Didn't you ever go back again?"

"Na," he said, blasé. "What for?"

I wondered about this. There just wasn't any amatory attraction there, that was obvious. I couldn't understand it, with a girl as appealing and magnetic as she'd seemed to me. But each one to his own inclinations I suppose, even at that age.

"What's her last name?" I asked. "You didn't give it."

"Her old man's name is Gaffney," he said.[4] "I know, because I've met him." I didn't know what he meant by that at first. Then he went on to explain: "She likes to call herself Hamilton, though; she says it was her grandmother's name and she's entitled to use it if she wants."

"Why?" I wondered.

"I danno; maybe she thinks it's classier."

I could understand that discontent with a name. I'd experienced it a little myself. I'd been fiercely proud of my surname always. Only, all through my boyhood I'd kept wishing they'd given me a curt and sturdier first name, something like the other boys had, "Jim" or "Tom" or "Jack," not "Cornell" a family name, originally). But it was too late to do anything about it now. The only improvement possible was by abbreviation. And even there I was handicapped. "Corny" was unappealing, even though the slang descriptive for "stale" hadn't yet come into use. "Connie" was unthinkable. All that was left was "Con," which always sounded flat to me for some reason.

"Hey!" he jeered explosively, belatedly becoming aware, I suppose, of the number of questions I'd been asking. "What happened? Did you get stuck on her already?"

"How could I have got stuck on her?" I protested uncomfortably. "I only just now met her."

But I knew I was lying; I knew I had.

The next evening, for the first time in a long time, I didn't stop by Frankie's place to have him come out with me. His company had suddenly become unwanted. Instead, I went around to Eighth Avenue by myself. As if to get my courage up sufficiently, I passed and repassed the doorway I had seen her go into, and finally took up my post in a closed-up store inset, across the way, and hopefully and watchfully began my first love-wait.

The love-wait—that sweet, and sometimes bittersweet, preliminary to each new meeting, which can be sanguine, sad, jealous, impatient, hurtful, angry, even end in a heated quarrel; and which I have sometimes thought has more in it of the true essence of the love affair—is the better part by far of the two, than the actual meeting itself that follows and ends it. For the latter is often humdrum, a let-down by comparison. Its opening remarks are certainly never brilliant, or even worth the making, most of the time. And the little things they say, and the little things they do, are quite commonplace after all, after the anticipatory reveries of the love-wait.

This love-wait can be carried out only by the boy or the man, for if the girl or the woman carries it out, she somehow detracts by just so much from it and from herself: from the desirability of meeting her, from the uncertainty as to whether she will appear or not, turning a mystic wistful expectancy, the borderline between absence and presence, into a flat, casual, commonplace meeting. Like the difference between a kiss and a handshake.

El trains would trundle by at intervals with a noise like low-volume thunder and cast strange parallelograms and Grecian-key friezes of light along the upper faces of the shrouded buildings, like the burning tatters of a kite's tail, streaming evenly along in the breezeless night. A little more often, one of the squared-off high-topped autos of the early Twenties would skirt over the gutters and through the enfilading iron girders that supported the structure above, with only an imminent collision to stop for, since there were no traffic lights yet this far uptown.

And on the sidewalks, more numerous still than either of the others, people on foot passed back and forth, as they'd always done on sidewalks, I suppose, since cities were first built, and as they'd continue to do long after the elevated trains and the high-topped cars were gone.

Once another girl showed up unexpectedly, and scurried up the few entrance-steps that led into the doorway, and I thought it was she, and almost started forward from where I was standing to sprint across the street and catch her before she went in. But then she stopped and turned for a moment, to say something to someone on the sidewalk behind her, and I saw her face and saw it wasn't, and sank back again upon my heels.

As the evening grew later, a sharp-edged wind sprang up, with the feel of cold rain in it. One of these supple, sinuous winds, able to round corners and make circles and eddies along the ground. It made me miserable, made me stamp my feet continuously and duck my chin down into the upturned collar of my coat, but I still wouldn't give up and go away. Until at last it was so late that I knew she wouldn't appear, or be able to linger with me if she did. Finally I turned and trudged off disconsolately, hands in pockets and downcast eyes on the sidewalk before me.

The following night the rain-threat of the night before had become an actuality, but that didn't keep me from my vigil. When you're eighteen and newly in love, what's rain? It didn't bother me as much as the wind had the night before, since it couldn't get into the niche of the store-entrance I had made my own, and the protective shed of the elevated-structure even kept the roadway of the street comparatively dry, though not the sidewalks, for there was an open canal above each one. The rain made the street seem gayer, not more dismal than it was at other times, for all these wet surfaces caught the lights more vividly and held them longer, as they went by. The rain was like an artist's palette, and these blobs of color, these smears of red and green and white and yellow and orange, hid the sooty grayness the street had in the light of day.

But at last I could see that, whatever the reason the night before, the weather would keep her in tonight. I had to turn and go away again, after standing a good deal less time.

The night after that, I reverted to my old habit and sought out Frankie. I wanted his advice. Or at least his reassurance that she actually did live there.

"Remember that girl you introduced me to couple days ago?" I blurted out almost as soon as we'd come out of his place.

"Vera? Sure," he said. "What about her?"

"Does she really live there, where you showed me?"

"Of course she does," he assured me. "Why would I lie about it?"

"Well, I hung around there all last night, and she never showed up, and I hung around all the night before—" I started to say it before I'd thought twice. I hadn't intended to tell him that part of it, but simply to find out if he'd seen her himself or knew her whereabouts. But once it was out, it was out, and too late to do anything about it. You're not anxious to tell even your closest friends about frustrations like that.

"In all that rain?" he chuckled, a wide grin overspreading his face.

"What's rain?" I said negligently.

This comment struck him as very funny, for some reason that I failed to see. He began to laugh uproariously, even bending over to slap himself on the kneecap, and he kept repeating incessantly: "Holy mackerel! Are *you* stuck on her! Waiting in the rain. No, you're not stuck on her, not much! Waiting in the rain."

"I wasn't *in* the rain," I corrected with cold dignity. "Maybe it was raining, but I wasn't *in* it."

I waited sullenly until his fit of (what I considered) tactless amusement had passed, then I suggested: "Let's go around there now, and see if we can see her. Maybe she's around there now." Why I would have been more likely to encounter her with him than alone, I wouldn't have been able to say. I think it was a case of misery wanting company.

When we'd reached the stepped-up entrance to her flat-building, we slung ourselves down onto the green-painted iron railing that bordered it, and perched there. We waited there like that for awhile, I uneasily, he stolidly. Finally, craning his neck and looking up the face of the building toward its topmost windows, which were impossible to make out at such a perspective, he stirred restlessly and complained: "This ain't going' get us nowhere. She may not come down all night. Go up and knock right on the door. That's the only way you'll get her to come down." He repeated the story of having once been up there himself, and what kindly disposed people he'd found her family to be.[5]

But this did nothing to overcome my timidity. "Not me," I kept repeating. "Nothing doing."

"Want me to come with you?" he finally offered, tired, I suppose, of being unable to get me to budge.

In one way I did and in one way I didn't. I wanted his moral support, his backing, desperately, but I didn't want him hanging around us afterward, turning it into a walking-party of three.

"Come part of the way," I finally compromised. "But stay back; if she comes to the door, don't let her see you."

So we walked inside the ground-floor hallway and started to trudge up the stairs, I in the lead, but of necessity rather than choice. We got to the fifth floor, and started up the last flight. He stopped eight or nine steps from the top. I had to go on up the short remaining distance alone, quailingly and queasily.

When I made the turn of the landing and reached the door, stopped, and just stood there looking at it.

"Go on, knock," he urged me in a hoarse whisper. "Don't just stand there."

I raised my hand as if measuring the distance it had to go, and then let it fall again.

"Go ahead. What's the matter with y'?" he hissed, hoarser and fiercer than before. He flung his arm up and then down again at me in utmost deprecation.

Again I raised my hand, touched the woodwork with it, let it fall back without striking. My knuckles had stage-fright; I couldn't get them to move.

Suddenly, before I knew what had happened, he bounded swiftly up the few remaining steps, whisked around the turn, and gave the door two heavy, massive thumps that (to my petrified ears, at least) sounded like cannon shots, the very opposite of what any signal of mine would be upon that particular door. Then he bounded back onto the stairs again, jolting down each flight with a sprightly but concussion-like jump that shook the whole stairwell. Before I had time to trace his defection (and perhaps turn around and go after him, as I was longing to do), the door had already opened and it was too late.

Vera's father stood there. Or at least, a middle-aged man did, and I assumed he was her father. He had on a gray woolen undershirt and a pair of trousers secured over it by suspenders. He must have been relaxing in a chair *en deshabille* when the knock disturbed him, for he was reslinging one of them over his shoulder as he stood there. He had a ruddy-complexioned face, and although he was by no means a good-looking man, he was a good-natured-looking one.

If he protruded somewhat in the middle, it was not excessively so, not more than to be expected in a man of his (to my young mind) multiplicity of years. He certainly was not corpulent. I would have stood there indefinitely, without being able to open my mouth, if he hadn't spoken first.

Frankie's bombastic retreat was still in progress, and the sound of it reached his ears.

"What's that going on down there?" he wanted to know. Stepping to the railing, he bent over and tried to peer down the well.

"It must be somebody on one of the lower floors in a hurry to go out," I said meekly. It was technically the truth anyway, even if a subterfuge of it.

Then Frankie gained the street, and silence descended once more.

Coming back to the door and turning to me, the man asked, with a sort of jovial severity, "Well, young fellow, and what can I do for you?"

After a swallow to wet my throat first, I managed to get out: "Excuse me, is Vera in?" And then added, somewhat redundantly: "I'm a friend of hers."

"Oh, are you now?" he said with chuckle. "Well, come on in, then. Glad to see you."

And before I realized it, I was on the inside, guided by his hand. The door had closed, and hundreds of her family seemed to be staring at me from all directions. Then the motes of momentary panic subsided in front of my eyes, and they condensed into no more than three or four people.

She wasn't there; I found that out almost at once. For the first moment or two I kept hoping she was merely out of sight in one of the other rooms, and would come in when she heard the increased tempo of their voices, but since she didn't, and they didn't call in to her, I finally had to resign myself to the fact that she wasn't in the flat at all. I'd have to face the music by myself as best I could.

In addition to her father, there were two other members of the family present; one was her mother, and the other presumably an aunt, but it took me some little time to differentiate between them. There was also a little girl in the room, of about nine or ten, whom they neglected to identify. I couldn't make out whether she was a smaller sister of Vera's, or the aunt's child, or just some neighbor's youngster given the freedom of the flat. In any case, at my advanced age I considered her beneath notice.

My impressions of her mother are not nearly as clear as they are of her father, possibly because he was the one who came to the door and whom I saw first, and without anyone else to distract my attention. I have a vague recollection of a tall but spare woman, with dark hair quite unlike Vera's, with an overtone of gray already about it at the outside, where it had a tendency to fuzz and fly up in gauzy little swatches that you could see the light through (the grayness therefore might have been only an illusion), and she would frequently put her hand to it and try to bring it back down to order, but it would never obey for long. Of the aunt, I have no surviving impressions whatever.

I sat down in the middle of all of them. They were probably actually spread about at random the way people usually are in a room, but it felt as if they were sitting around me in a complete circle, eying me critically and weighing me in the balance. I felt very constrained and ill at ease, and kept wishing I could sink through the floor, chair and all. It had been the worst possible timing on my part, too, I kept telling myself. If I'd just waited a few minutes longer and not listened to Frankie, I could have met Vera by herself, intercepted her when she came back and kept out of all this.

I'd already been smoking, sparingly but steadily, for some months past, and I'd already found it to be good as a bracer in moments of difficulty or stress. There was a package in my pocket right as I sat there, but I was afraid to take it out in front of them. I wanted to make a good impression, and I cannily told myself that if they thought me too knowing or advanced for my years they might discourage my trying to see any more of her.

As soon as I'd given my name, her father said: "Oh, sure. Con, is that you? We've heard about you from Veronica."

(He called her Veronica, I noticed, never Vera. I couldn't, if I'd wanted to; there was something too stiff and distant about the name.)

And her mother, nodding approvingly, added: "Yes, she told us about meeting you."

Hearing this made me feel quite good, though it did nothing to alleviate my present misery. It showed she was interested, if nothing else, and it augured well for the future.

The next and natural question from her father was, what did I do, what sort of work?

I told him, with a slight touch of contrition, that I was going to college. This seemed to impress him, to my surprise. I had thought they might turn up their noses at me for not being an honest working-man. "Are you, now?" he said. "A college sthudent."

"I'm just a first-year man," I explained, again a little penitently.[6] I had had impressed on my mind only too well the low opinion held about us by upperclassmen. "Freshman class, Frosh they call us. Then after that come sophomores. Then juniors. Then you're a senior."

Vera's mother clucked her tongue at this, and I wasn't quite sure how to translate the little sound accurately. I think it was intended as sympathy for all that hard work ahead.

"And what are you taking up?" her father asked. "What are you going to be after you get out?"

"Journalism," I said. "I want to be a writer."[7]

"That's a hard job," he said forebodingly.

I tried to explain that I meant free-lance writing and not newspaper writing, that I was just majoring in journalism because that was the closest thing to it. But he didn't seem to follow that too well; he seemed content to remain with his original conception. And turning to Vera's mother, he said, "I think that's the first college sthudent Veronica's ever known, isn't it?"

She tactfully interposed: "Well, she's very young yet."

In the meantime, in spite of the conversation having been an easy one to carry on, since it had dealt exclusively with me, I kept wondering what there would be to talk about next, once this topic was over, and hoping that another elevated train would go clattering by momentarily and bring me a brief respite. It would be impossible to continue a conversation until after the front windows had stopped rattling. But none did. It seemed as though, just when you wanted them, they became few and far between.

At this point there was a twitching-about of the doorknob from the outside, the door was pushed open, and Vera came in. She'd evidently been to the store for groceries. She hugged two very large brown paper bags in one arm, and since these came up past one side of her face and hid it, she did not see me at first.

She rounded her cheeks, blew out her breath, and said something about the stairs. That they were enough to kill you, I think it was. But in a good-natured, not ill-humored way. She closed the door by pushing a heel back against it, without turning.

I remember thinking how graceful and debonaire was the little flirt and swirl this movement created in the loose-hanging checked coat she had on, as I watched her do it. Then she turned her head suddenly, so that the obscuring bags were swept to one side, and saw me.

"Con!" she said, in a high-pitched voice that was almost a little scream. She nearly dropped the columnar bags, but reclasped them just in time. "How did you get up here?"

"I walked up," I answered in perfect seriousness, without stopping to think, and they all laughed at that, herself included, as though I'd intended it to be very funny.

"I never thought I'd find *you* up here," she said next. "You're the last one!"

I wasn't sure what she meant by that; and afraid that, if I asked her, the answer might turn out to be unwelcome, I didn't ask.

"How did you know where it was?" she went on. "How did you know this was the right place?"

My instinct told me it might not be in my own best interest to bring Frankie's name into this, or recall him to her mind any more than was strictly necessary. She'd known him before she had me, after all. So I simply and untruthfully said: "I asked somebody in the house," and that seemed to content her.

I had a fleeting impression, as I watched her expression and listened to the intonation of what she was saying to me, that she was enjoying, rather than otherwise, having her entire family as spectators to this little meeting of ours, and auditors to its accompanying dialogue, liked having their attention fixed on her the way it was. But if *she* enjoyed it, I didn't, quite the opposite, and this nerved me to summon up courage to come out with what had brought me up there in the first place.

"Vera," I said nervously, "would you like to come for a walk with me?"

She didn't answer directly, but said "Wait'll I take these back where they belong first," and picking up the two cumbersome bags, which she had set down upon a table, she left the room with them. She was gone for some time, longer than would have been necessary simply to carry them back to the kitchen and set them down there, so I began to imagine she had stopped off in her own room on the way, to tidy her hair or something of the sort. Then when she came back, I saw that she had removed both the checked coat and the tamoshanter she had been wearing, and my hopes were dashed.

After a lame pause, I finally asked her a second time: "Vera, wouldn't you like to come for a walk?"

"I don't know if I can," she said, and I saw her exchange a look with her mother.

The latter remarked cryptically, "You run along. I'll do them for you tonight, and you can do them tomorrow night instead."

Whereupon Vera hurried back inside again, throwing me an auspicious "I'll be ready in a minute, Con," over her shoulder, and this time, when she returned, was once more in coat and tamoshanter, and ready to leave.

I said the required polite and stilted good-byes, she opened the door, and a minute later we were free and by ourselves on the other side of it.

"It was my turn to do the dishes tonight," she told me as we went scrabbling down the stairs, she running her hand along the bannister railing, I on the outside with her other hand in mine.

The moment we were by ourselves, the moment the door had closed behind us, perfect ease and naturalness came back to me again, and to Vera too, though she hadn't felt herself to be on exhibition as I had: One didn't have to weigh one's words, they just came flowing out in any kind of order, and yet inevitably they were the right words, without the trouble of trying to make them so beforehand. One didn't have to execute each smallest move or gesture twice, once in the mind and once in the actuality, they too flowed unchecked in perfect unstudiedness. There were no questions that required answers, none were put and none were given, there were just confidences streaming out and blending.

And I remember wondering at the time why this should be, for they had been amiable enough, her people, hadn't been unfriendly, had tried to make me feel at ease, and yet they hadn't been able to. I think I know now: it wasn't because we were a boy and girl who were interested in each other that we felt this lack of constraint the moment we were away from them, it was because we were both of the same generation, and they were not.

There is an insurmountable wall, a barrier, between each generation, especially in the earlier stages of life. Children are so cut off from the grown-up world they are almost a species apart, a different breed of creature than the rest of the race. Very young people of our age, hers and mine, have no interests whatever in common with those who are in the next age group. Then as we progress up through the thirties, the barrier becomes less and less, until finally it has melted away altogether, and everyone is middle-aged alike. Twenty-five and forty-five seem alike to us now. But by that time a new barrier has formed, at the back instead of the front, and new very young are once more walled off from those who, only yesterday, were the very young themselves.

I asked her if she wanted to see a movie.

"No," she said. "Let's just walk instead. I saw the one at the Morningside a couple of days ago, and they haven't changed it yet."[8]

We stopped in first at an ice-cream parlor on the corner of 116th Street. This had little tables separated from each other by lattices, up which clambered waxed-linen leaves and cretonne flowers. It also had an electric player piano at the back, forerunner of the later jukeboxes, and arched festoons of small, gaily colored light bulbs, curved like arabesques across the ceiling. There was a marble-topped soda fountain running the length of it at one side, but we sat down opposite one another at one of the little tables.

She made a selection, and I followed suit and ordered what she had.

These were called banana splits, as far as I can recall.[9] They were served in oblong glass receptacles with stems on them, for no ordinary-sized dish could have held everything that went into them. The holder was lined first with two half bananas, sliced lengthwise. On top of these were placed three mounds of ice cream in a row, green, white and pink. Over these in turn was poured a chocolate syrup. Next were added chunks of pineapple and a sprinkling of chopped or grated nuts. The whole thing was surmounted by a feathery puff of whipped cream, and into this was stuck a maraschino cherry, dyeing the whipped cream red around it.

Beside each of these, for obvious reasons, was placed a glass of plain water.

That we found this concoction not only edible but even immensely enjoyable is only another illustration of the differences there are between the generations.

When we got up I left a tip on the table, more to impress her than for the sake of the waiter. I saw her eyes rest on it for a moment, as I had hoped they would.

After we left there, we walked over to Morningside Park, and through it along a softly lamplit pathway. It is a long but narrow park, no more than a block in depth at any point. That part of New York is built on two levels, and Morningside Heights, which runs along the western edge of the park, is perched high above Morningside Drive, which runs along the eastern edge. From it you can overlook all that part of the city which lies to the eastward, its rooftops and its lights.[10]

We walked along slowly, our hands lightly linked and swinging low between us. I began to whistle "Kalua," which had just come out a little while before, and after awhile she accompanied me by humming it along with me.[11] For years, whenever I heard "Kalua," it brought back that first walk I took with her, and I could feel her fingers lightly twined in mine again, and see the lamplight falling over us again in blurry patches like slowly sifted, softly falling cornmeal.

She asked me where I lived, myself. I told her One Hundred and Thirteenth Street.

"We're just a block apart," she noted. "Only, on different sides of the park."

But New York then, in its residential zoning, was a snobbish, stratified sort of town, and the park did more than divide it physically, it divided it economically as well.[12] That, however, was of no concern to us. That applied only to our elders.

We climbed the wide, easily sloping stairs that led to the upper level and came out at 116th Street, at that little rotunda with its bas-reliefs and circular stone seat-rest,[13] and stood there awhile, taking in the spread of the city's lights below and outward from us, until the eye couldn't follow them any more, and lost them in the reaches of the night. But the young haven't too much time to spend on mere inanimate beauty, they're too immediately interested in each other.

We turned away and walked down Morningside Heights a block or two, and opposite, where there was a little French church standing, called Notre Dame de Lourdes, I think.[14] We sat down together on a bench without saying a word, and moved close.

And from that night on, whenever we met, we always met at that one particular bench and never any other. I used to wonder at times, later, who had been sitting there after we did, who had met there once we stopped going to it, and if they were young like we were, and if they were happy; what *their* stories were, and how they turned out in the end. They never knew about us, we never knew about them. For park benches can't talk.

We kissed, and nestled close, and (I suppose) laughed together about something now and then. The pattern never changes throughout time. Then presently and very tentatively I crossed the line from the innocuous to the more innate.

The first time she let it pass unnoticed, either not wanting to seem too edgy and ready to take offense, or else mistakenly thinking it had been unintentional and the wiser thing to do was not to call attention to it; and I, misconstruing, repeated it. This time she caught my hand and held it fast, but in such a minor-keyed way that it is difficult to put it into exact words. For she didn't brush it off or fling it aside peremptorily, but held it still with hers, almost where it had been but not quite, so that her gesture couldn't be mistaken for collaboration, only for the deterrent it was.

"Don't do that," she said in a low-spoken voice that was all the more inflexible for that reason. "I'll get up from here if you do."

"And I don't want to," she went on after a moment. "I like you, and I like being here with you."

I kept quiet, feeling that it was not up to me to do the talking. And even if it had been, not knowing what there would have been to say, the thing was so self-explanatory. In my own mind I unjustly put her into the position of having to excuse or at least explain herself, when it should have been the other way around. But she seemed to accept the role without questioning its fairness.

"I know how some girls feel about it,"   she said thoughtfully. " 'Oh, it's just this once, with this one boy. Then it'll never happen again.' But it does happen again. If you didn't stop the first time, then you never will the second. And before you know, it's with another boy. And then another boy. And pretty soon, with *any* boy at all."

Made uncomfortable, I gave a slight pull to my hand, and she released it, and I drew it away.

"I want to get married some day," she explained. "And when I do, I don't want to have anything to hide." And tracing the point of her shoe thoughtfully along the ground in little patterns and watching it as she did so, she went on: "I wouldn't want to stand up in a church, and know that somewhere some other man was laughing at my husband behind his back. I wouldn't be entitled to wear a bridal veil, it would be a lie before God." Then she asked me point blank: "Would you want to marry somebody that had been with everybody else before that?"

She stopped and waited for my answer.

I hated to have to give her the answer, because it vindicated her own argument so.

"No," I said grudgingly, at last.

I wondered if her mother had instilled this into her, if they had had a talk about it, for it must have come from somewhere to be so strong and clear-sighted in her, but I didn't think it was right to openly ask her.

But almost as if she had read my mind, she added: "I don't need anybody else to tell me. I've had it all thought out from the time I was fourteen, already. From the time I first knew about things like that. Or knew a little about them, anyway. I made up my mind that when I got older, no matter how much I cared for a fellow, it wasn't going to be that way.

"It don't have to be that way," she reiterated unshakable. "No matter how much in love a girl and a fellow are, it still don't have to be that way."

I remember thinking that, as she spoke, the slight dent in the grammar only added to, didn't detract from, the beautiful sincerity of her conviction.

I looked at her in a new way now, commending her, esteeming her, for the values she adhered to. Nineteen is basically idealistic, far more than the after-years are, and in spite of its young blood would rather have an ideal it can look up to, that keeps itself just beyond reach of the everyday grubbing fingers.[15]

She probably translated the look. I saw her smile with quiet contentment, as if that were the way she had hoped to be looked at. Then, as if to make up for any crestfallenness I might have felt, she stroked me lightly but affectionately along the side of the face with the tips of her fingers. And bunching her lips and poising them, commanded me winningly, "Now let me have a kiss."

After I'd taken her back to her own door and then gone home myself, I thought about it. I'd been very intent in the first place: I could tell that easily enough, as I took off my clothing piece by piece to get ready for bed. But that wasn't the important thing, that was just a reflex, little better than a muscle-spasm. I sat down in a chair first, to quiet down before I tried to sleep, and I turned the whole thing over in my mind.

The important thing about her refusal was the vastly longer term of life and the far more indelible imprint it gave to our relationship. It changed what would have been an overnight thing into a more or less permanent affinity, at least as far as the foreseeable future was concerned. On the one hand there would have been a few short weeks of furtive, overheated meetings, and then oblivion. No name to remember, no face to recall. On the other hand, there were an uncurtailed succession of joyous, daily encounters, sprightly, open and unashamed, and though immature perhaps, in every sense a budding love affair. And an imperishable print on the memory. She stayed with me ever since. I still remember her name, and some of the things she said, and some of the clothes she wore, and some of the ways she looked. There's a sort of inverse ratio at work there.

Women, even very young girl-women (which amounts to the same thing), must walk a precarious tightrope. If they fall off, into somebody's waiting arms, they almost always lose him in the end. If they stay on, even though he's been kept at a distance, they capture some part of him.

I think I dimly sensed this to some extent, even that very first night as I sat there and thought it over. But if I didn't then, I certainly realize it now, as I look back from forty years away. For I must have had some girl fully, must have had my first girl fully, then or not long after. But not a trace of recollection remains.[16] Yet Vera still stays in my mind. The very fact that I'm writing this is proof enough of that.

That first-night incident on the bench set the whole pattern from then on for our little sentimental interlude. (And I suppose it was little, but it was a valid one nevertheless; seventeen and nineteen can't have a bravura romance.) It was understood between us without speaking about it any further, it was crystallized, that that was the way it was going to be. And that was the way it was. And I myself wanted it that way now just as much as she did. She personified that to me now, she was its identification. She wore a halo, as far as I was concerned. Youthful and jaunty and informal, but a halo just the same.

We met every day from then on, without missing one. But not always at the same time. For my schedule of classes was zig-zag, no two days alike, and since it was all Greek to her anyway, no matter how often I tried to have her memorize it, she always got to the bench before I did in order to be sure to be on time.

I'd see her doll-sized figure from a distance. As I came closer she'd jump to her feet and fling her arms wide in pantomimic welcome, while I'd break into a headlong run, and as I reached her, I tossed my books carelessly over to the side in order to have both arms free for the hug that would follow.

There was something of the antic in this. We both recognized it and we both would have been willing to admit it. But the underlying emotion was bonafide enough; it was just that we didn't know how to handle it, so we parodied it. If we were too young to actually be in love, to know how to be in love, then we were certainly smitten with one another, infatuated with one another, that much was sure.

We'd sit there for hours sometimes, oblivious of the needling cold, huddled closely together, sometimes my coat around the two of us, our breaths forming bladder-shapes of vapor like the dialogue-balloons cartoonists draw coming out of their characters' mouths.

We talked a lot. I don't remember about what; the language of the young. You forget that language very quickly; within a few short years it's a foreign tongue, the knack for it is completely gone. Sometimes, though, we were quiet and tenderly pensive.

I used to get home at all hours. I ate alone almost every night now; everyone else had usually finished by the time I showed up. But I'd find something put aside and kept warm for me. What it was I never knew half the time, I was so wrapped up in retrospect repetitions of what had just taken place. I don't recall that my family ever voiced any remonstrances about it. They seem to have been very lenient in this respect. Maybe being the only male, even though a very unseasoned one, in a household of two doting women had something to do with it.[17]

This routine went on daily for about two or three months, as the season began its final climb to the holidays at the top of the year and 1922 slowly blended into 1923. Then a fly landed in the honey, from a totally unexpected quarter. I came home one evening and my mother remarked: "Hetty Lambert called up today while you were out."

This was a life-long friend of my mother's. They had been schoolgirl chums, and the intimacy had continued uninterrupted into the married lives of both. Hetty had been well-to-do in her own right even as a youngster (my mother had told me), and she had married a man in the silk-import business who was in turn exceedingly well off,[18] so she must have been a very wealthy woman.

For my part, from my pre-twenty point of view, I found her musty and dowdy. When she wasn't spending whole mornings clipping coupons in a bank vault, she was spending afternoons visiting with her dead in the family mausoleum. Their one recreation, she and her husband, was a lifetime box at the Metropolitan Opera, but since he invariably fell asleep in it, even that was wasted. She used to do her own marketing for the table personally, squeezing produce, with an elderly chauffeur following her around with a basket to put them in, and if she thought the weight was a bit short or the price a few cents too high she would fume to the high heavens, until they let her have it her way for the sake of peace and quiet.

"What'd she have to say?" I said, totally uninterested but dutifully willing to appear to listen for the sake of the high regard my mother seemed to hold her in.

"Thursday of next week is her daughter's birthday. Janet's giving a little party for her friends, and she wants you to come."

"Oh, no I'm not!" I promptly burst out. "That's the last place I'm going. You don't get me there, not on your life!" And so on, at great length.

"I don't see why you feel that way," my mother remonstrated mildly, when I had finally come to a stop. "You've gone every year, since you were both children. You went last year."

"Last year was different." Meaning I'd been a year younger then. And mainly, I hadn't known Vera then.

Then, perhaps thinking this might be an added inducement, she went on reassuringly: "Hetty and her husband aren't going to be there. They're going out for the evening, and turning over the whole apartment to Janet and her friends."

But this was no inducement whatever as far as I was concerned. I found Janet about as appealing—romantically speaking—as an overstuffed chair with broken-down springs, whether her mother was present or not. No mutual dislike felt by two boys toward one another (or by two girls toward one another, for that matter) can ever quite equal in wholehearted intensity the very occasional and very rare dislike felt toward one another by a boy *and* girl, when it does happen to come along. And that was the case with us. We had a beautiful, inbred ill will toward one another, due most likely to having been thrown so constantly at each other's heads when we were both small children.

There wasn't a thing about her that suited me. Her laugh resembled a sneer. Her most inconsequential remark had a cutting edge, but you only realized it sometime after the cuticle had slowly started peeling back. Her clothes were probably costly, but she always managed to do something to them that spoiled the looks of them. Just by being in them, I guess. Her manners weren't bad, for only one reason. She didn't have any at all. She was the only young girl I had ever seen who crumbled her rolls up into pieces at a dinner-party table and then threw them at every boy around her. Not just momentarily, but throughout each and every course, until they became miserable trying to eat without getting hit.

Even the way she kissed was a form of snobbish superiority. She didn't kiss with her mouth at all. She tilted her nose in the air and pushed her cheek up against the recipient somewhere just below the eardrum. I hadn't kissed her since we were twelve, but I had watched her kiss her mother and her older married sister, and she did it that way even with them.

All in all, though it was difficult for me then (and now) to find an exact verbal synonym for the word "brat," a pictorial one was easy to come by. It was simply Janet. She was the perfect spoiled rich brat.

"You'll have to call her up, one way or the other," my mother said, still trying to persuade me. "You can't just ignore it. Even if you're not fond of Janet," she pointed out, "you may have a good time. There may be somebody there you'll like."

A sudden inspiration hit me. You bet there will be somebody there I like, I promised myself. I'll see to it that there is!

I made the courtesy call back, as required. The maid answered first, and then called Janet to the phone.

"'Lo," Janet said, in that sulky voice that was a characteristic of hers.

"'Lo," I answered, equally uncordial.

Neither of us ever used our given names to one another any more than was strictly necessary; another sign of fondness.

"Are you coming?" she asked briefly.

"Yeah," I answered. Then my voice took on an added degree of animation. "Listen," I said.

"What?" she asked, as lifeless as ever.

"Can I bring somebody with me?"

"A boy?" she asked, and her voice perked up a little.

"Nah, not a boy," I said disgustedly. Who'd ever heard of taking another fellow along with you to a party? "A girl."

"Oh," she said, and her voice deflated again. Then after a moment's reflection she agreed, without any great show of enthusiasm. "I s'pose so. There was one girl short at the table, anyhow."

I couldn't wait to tell Vera about it. I came rushing up to the bench the following day, kissed her breathlessly and for once almost perfunctorily, and pulling her down onto the bench along with me, blurted out: "Know what? We've been invited to a party."

But to my surprise, instead of being pleased, she acted appalled about it at first. "Where is it?" she asked, and when I'd told her, she kept repeating almost hypnotically, "But *Riverside Drive*! I can't go *there*."

"What's so wonderful about Riverside Drive?" I said, shrugging uncomprehendingly. "I've been to their place lots of times. In the wintertime they get all the ice-cold wind blowing in from the river. And in the summer, when it *would* be cooler than other parts of town, they're not there to enjoy it anyway."

But temperature wasn't the deterrent, some kind of monetary denominator—or differential—was. Her mind evidently magnified it and couldn't rid itself of the fixed idea. I had never taken this into account myself, so I wasn't in a position to see her point of view.

"That isn't what I mean!" she said impatiently. "Only rich people live there."

"What difference does it make?" I said. "You're going with *me*. You're not worried about *me*, are you? Then why worry about them?"

"But you're different," she said, groping to find the right words. "I never think about you in that way, maybe because I'm used to you. You're *friendly*, and you never seem to dress up much. And besides, you're a fellow, and it's not the fellows that worry me as much as it is the girls."

"What about them? They're a bunch of drips. You've got more real personality than all of them put together," I said loyally.

But I couldn't seem to overcome her misgivings.

"And what about a dress? What kind are they going to wear?"
"I d'no," I said vaguely. "Dresses for dancing in, I guess. Haven't you got one of those?"

"When do I go dancing?" she said, almost resentfully.

When we separated that evening, I still hadn't been able to bring her to the point of agreeing to come. The most I could get her to say was "I'll think it over, and I'll let you know."

The next time we met it was the same thing, and the time after. As far as I could judge her attitude, it wasn't coyness or wanting to be coaxed. She seemed attracted to the idea of going, and yet at the same time something seemed to keep holding her back. One time she even made the outrageous suggestion: "I'll walk down there with you as far as the door, and then you go in by yourself. I could even meet you later, after you leave." Then before I had time for the heated protest that I felt this deserved, she quickly recanted it, saying "No, that would be foolish, wouldn't it?"

I finally told her, another time, "Let's forget about it. If you're not going, then I'm not either. Who needs the party?"

But she wouldn't hear of this either. "No, I'm not going to dish you out of the party. You're expected there, and if you don't show up, I'll get the blame. You'll have to go. I won't meet you that night, I won't come out at all, so if you don't go, you'll be all by yourself."

"We go together, or we stay away together," I insisted stubbornly, as I had right along.

This went on for nearly the whole week or eight days preceding the controversial little event. Then on the very night before, after I'd already just about given up all further hope of persuading her and was ready to quit trying once and for all, she suddenly said—not at the very first, but after we'd been sitting there together for quite some time— "I'm going to tell you something that'll please you. Want to hear it?"

I told her sure, sure I did.

"I'm going with you tomorrow night."

I bounced to my feet, took hold of her two hands in my two, and swung them vigorously in and out, to give vent to my elation.

"I made up my mind several days ago," she admitted, smiling at my enthusiasm, "but I didn't tell you until now because I wanted to keep it as a surprise."

The dinner had been set for "somewhere between seven-thirty and eight" (Janet's words), so we arranged to meet three-quarters of an hour earlier, in order to give ourselves time enough to get there without hurrying. She told me to wait for her at the bench, she'd come there, and I gave in to that readily enough. I didn't like the idea of having to pass in review before her whole family, anyway.

By six-fifteen the following evening, all aglow, I'd completed my rather uncomplicated toilette, which included the by-now semi-weekly rite of a light overall shave, more in tribute to the future than a present necessity, and put on my one dark blue suit. I stopped in to see my mother for a minute, before leaving.

"Are you taking her anything?" she asked me. "Because I have a little unopened bottle of cologne you could have. It would save you the expense of buying something."

"I'll pick her up a box of candy on the way," I said evasively. I knew I wouldn't; I didn't think that much of Janet.

"I'd like to take her a baseball bat, and give it to her over the head!"
I added darkly.

She was laughing, accommodatingly but a little unsurely, as I left
her.

I was ahead of time, Vera wasn't there yet, when I got to the bench.

I sat down to wait for her, and at first I whistled and was relaxed,
one knee cocked up high in front of me and my hands locked around
it. But the minutes came, the minutes went, more minutes came, more
went, and still she didn't arrive. Pretty soon I wasn't carefree any more,
I was on needles and pins. I turned and I twisted and I shifted; I constantly
changed position, as though by doing that I would bring her there faster.
I crossed my legs over one way, then over the other. I swung my hoisted
foot like a pendulum. I drummed the bench-seat with my fingers like
the ticking away of a fast-moving taxi meter. I raked my nails through
my hair, wrecking its laboriously achieved sleekness. I clasped my hands
at the back of my neck and let my elbows hang from there. I probably
smoked more than in any comparable length of time up to that point
in my short young life.

I even combined two positions into one, so to speak—the sitting
and the standing—using the top of the bench-back for a seat and planting
my feet on the seat itself.

It was while I was in this last hybrid position that I heard a skittering
sound, like raindrops spattering leaves, and a small figure came rushing
out of the lamp-spiked darkness toward me. A figure smaller than Vera,
anyway. It was the little girl who'd been up in the flat that first day
I went there, and who seemed to tag around after Vera a good deal.
I'd glimpsed her more than once hanging around, helping Vera pass
the time while she was waiting for me on the bench, and then when
I came along she'd discreetly drift off, probably at a confidential word
from Vera.

She seemed to have run all the way, judging by her breathlessness;
it was no inconsiderable distance for a youngster her size. Or maybe
it was only feasible for that very reason, because of her young age.

"What happened?" I asked, hopping down from the bench-back.
"Why didn't she meet me here like she said she was going to?"

But she only repeated verbatim the message she had been given,
evidently having been told nothing else. "She says come right away.
She's waiting for you at her house."

I bolted off without even giving the poor little thing time to stand
still a minute and catch her breath. She turned and faithfully started
back the way she had just come, following me. But my long legs soon
outdistanced her shorter ones, and after falling behind more and more,
she finally bleated out: "Don't go so fast! I can't keep up with you!"

I stopped a couple of times to let her catch up, but finally I shouted back to her, rather unfeelingly: "You're holding me up! I can't stand and wait for you each time. Come back by yourself!" And I sprinted off and soon left her completely behind.

When I got to the building that housed Vera's flat, I ran up the whole six flights without a pause even at landings—but if you can't do it at that age, then you never can do it at all—and finally, half suffocating, I rapped on the door with tactful restraint (remembering the terrible thump Frankie had given it that first day, and trying not to repeat it).

The door opened, but there was no one standing there alongside it. Then Vera's voice said, from in back of it: "Come on in, but keep walking straight ahead and don't turn your head. Hold your hands over your eyes."

I thought, for a minute, she hadn't finished dressing yet, and wondered why she'd admitted me so quickly, in that case. I heard her close the door.

Then she said: "Now you can turn. But don't look yet."

Obediently I turned, eyelids puckered up, exaggeratedly tight, as though normal closing in itself wasn't a sufficient guarantee.

"*Now!*" she said triumphantly. "Now look."

I opened my eyes and looked, and she was all dressed up for the party.

"How do you like me?" she asked eagerly.

It was blue, I'm almost sure. I *was* sure then, but I'm not sure now any more. But I think it must have been blue. She was a blonde, and it would have been blue more likely than anything else.

"My aunt ran it up for me on her machine," she went on breathlessly. "We bought the material at Koch's, on a-Hunner-Twenty-fifth.[19] We only needed four yards, and we even had some left over for a lampshade when we got through."

Looking at it, I could well believe it. They were wearing them short and skimpy that year.

"But that isn't all I've got to show you. Just wait'll you see this!"

She went hurrying into one of the other rooms, a bedroom, I guess, and then paper crackled in there. It didn't rustle softly, as tissue paper would have; it crackled sharply, more as stiff brown wrapping paper would.

Then she came back, something swirling blurrily about her as it settled into place.

"What've you got to say now!" she cried.

The blue party-shift had disappeared from view, and she had glossy fur wrapped all around her, covering her everywhere, except her face and legs. She was hugging it tight to her, caressing it, luxuriating in it, in a way I can't describe. I'd never seen a girl act that way over something inanimate before. She even tilted her head and stroked one cheek back and forth against it, over and over and over again. She made love to it, that's about all I can say.

I don't know what kind it was. I didn't know anything about furs, then. Years later, when it had gotten so that I could identify mink, simply by dint of constant sight-references ("Mink," somebody would say, and then I would look at it), I realized in retrospect that whatever it had been, it hadn't been mink. It hadn't been that dark a shade of brown. It had been more a honey-colored kind of brown. Anyway:

"Holy mackerel!" I cried in excitement, or something equally fatuous but equally sincere, and I took a step backward in a parody of going off balance that was only partly pretense.

She kept turning from side to side, and then pivoting all the way around like a professional model, showing it to me from all angles. Her little eyebrows were arched in the cutest expression of mimic hauteur I'd ever seen then or ever have since.

"But it must have cost a pile of money," I said anxiously. "How'd you ever get them to...?"

"Oh, it's not all paid for," she said facilely. "We made a down payment on it, and they let us take it home on approval. If we're not satisfied we can return it, and they'll give us our money back."

"I didn't know they did that with fur coats," I said, impressed. But then I didn't know much about the fur-coat traffic anyway. "It's the cat's meow," I said, which was the utmost you could give to anything in commendation.

We kissed, I in ecstatic admiration, she in jubilant satisfaction at being so admired. "Don't spoil my mouth, now," she cautioned, but even that didn't mar the kiss, for though she withheld her lips protectively from mine, she held my head between her two hands in affectionate pressure.

"We all set, now?" I asked.

"Just one thing more," she said. She produced a tiny glass vial, not much thicker than a toothpick, and uncapped it. She stroked herself with it at several preordained places: at the base of her throat and in back of both ears. "Woolworth's," she said. "But it's good stuff. You only get a couple of drops for twenty-five cents."

It smelled very good to me, that was all I knew. Like a hundred different flowers ground up into a paste and leavened with honey.

"Don't let me forget to turn out all the lights," she said with a final look around. "They'll raise Cain if I do. It costs like the devil when you leave the electh-tricity on all night." I remember how she said it. That was how she said it. Electh-tricity. It sounded even better than the right way.

That taken care of, we closed the door after us and went rattling down the stairs, on our way at last.

"Have you got a key for when you come home, or will you have to wake them up?" I asked her on the way down.

"My aunt gave me hers for tonight," she said. "I don't think they'll be back until after we are. They went to a wake, and you know how long those things last."

I didn't, but I nodded knowingly, so she wouldn't know I didn't.

When we reached the street-entrance, she stopped short, and even seemed to shrink back within its recesses for a moment, almost as though she were afraid to come out into the open, you might say. "How're we going down there?" she asked.

"Why, in a taxi, of course," I answered loftily. "I wouldn't take you any other way, dressed the way you are."

"Well then you go out ahead and get one, and bring it back to the door with you," she said. "I'll wait inside here until you do. I don't want any of the neighbors to see me standing around on the sidewalk dressed like this. Then by tomorrow, it'll be all over the house."

"What's that their business?" I asked truculently, but I went ahead and did what she'd suggested.

I got one about a block away, got in, and rode back to the doorway in it. Then I got out and held the door open for Vera.

There was a moment's wait, like when you're gathering yourself together to make a break for it. Then Vera came rushing out headlong and scurried in. I never saw anyone get into a waiting taxi so fast. She was like a little furry animal scampering for cover.

She pushed herself all the way over into the corner of the seat, out of sight. "Put the light out," she whispered urgently.

The closing of the door, as I got in after her, cut it off automatically. I heard her give a deep, heartfelt sigh as it went out, and thought it was probably one of contentment because we were finally on the last lap of our way to the party.

I told the driver Janet's address, and we started off, she and I clasping hands together on the seat between us.

The lights came at us and went by like shining volleyballs rolling down a bowling alley, and it was great to be young, and to be sitting next to your girl in a hustling taxi, and to be going to a party with her. It's never so much fun in your whole life afterwards as it is that first time of all.

I remember thinking: this is only the beginning. I'll go to other parties with Vera, like this. Every party I ever go to from now on, I'll go to only with Vera.

I can no longer recall too many of the particulars of the party, at this distance, just its overall generalities. It was about average for its time and for its age group, I guess; like any other party then, and probably still pretty much like any such party now, given a few insignificant variations in tricks of dress and turns of dance and turns of speech. The basic factor remains the same: the initial skirmishing of very young men and girls in preparation for the pairing off of later life. Learning the rules for later on. The not-quite-fully mature, trying to act the part of grown-ups. No, that's not wholly accurate, either. For we were enclosed in our own world, and therefore we *were* what we seemed to ourselves to be, in every sense of the word. We reacted to one another on that plane, and that made it a fact. Those outside that world were not the real grown-ups, they were simply aliens, and their viewpoint had no validity among us. The wall of the generations.

She had a fleeting moment or two of uncertainty, of faltering self-confidence, as we stood facing the door, waiting for it to be opened. I could tell it by the whiteness of her face, by the strained fixity of her eyes. Then as the room spread itself out before us like a slowly opening, luminous, yellow and ivory fan, alive with moving figures and flecks of disparate color—the party—her lack of assurance passed and she swept forward buoyantly, almost with a lilt to her step, not more than two or three fingers lightly touching the turn of my arm in token indication that I was her escort. And from then on, all the rest of the evening, that was the word to describe her: buoyant. Whether she was standing or sitting still, dancing or just moving about without music; whatever she was doing. She seemed to skim over the floor instead of being held to it like the rest of us.

She was well liked at once, it was easy to see that. All the very first words that followed my pronunciation of her name each time were warm and friendly and interested and showed a real eagerness on the speaker's part to become better acquainted with her, over and above the formal politeness that the occasion indicated. We weren't much on formal politeness anyway, at our ages.

I had expected the boys to like her, but the girls very patently did too. For a boy will like almost any girl except the most objectionable, that's part of his make-up, but to be liked by her own kind is the real test of popularity for a girl. Within an hour or two of the start of the affair, Vera was a beckoned-to and sought-after and arms-about-waists member of each successive little group and coterie that went inside to the bedroom to giggle and chatter and powder its collective noses away from the boys for a few moments' respite. She was as incandescent as a lighted lamp swinging from the ceiling of an old-fashioned ship's cabin and darting its rays into the farthest corners.

But Janet was the big surprise of it all. I had fully expected he
to be her usual prickly self, and though for my own part this wouldn't
have fazed me in the least (I even welcomed it, for it put us on a more
even footing of mutual ill will, of verbal give-and-take with no holds
barred), I had intended to do all I could to protect Vera from her quills.
But it turned out not to be necessary at all. Janet seemed to take to
her from the moment that she first stepped forward to welcome her,
sizing her up in one quick, comprehensive, head-to-foot look, the kind
even very young girls her age are fully capable of giving. She obviously
liked her, whatever her reasons. From then on, she made her the exception
to the entire group. She was quite simple, natural, unaffected, cordial
and hospitable toward her, with just a touch of self-effacement. Her
smiles were elfin, but at least they were real smiles. Her remarks had
no rusty razor blades imbedded in them. A new Janet I had never seen
before began to peer shyly forth.

I caught myself thinking as I watched her: Well, I'll be darned.
Sometimes you know people for years, and then suddenly you find out
you don't really know them at all. Somebody new comes along who
brings out another side to them that you didn't even suspect was there,
simply because it never had been shown to you before. This is how
she would be if she had really liked anyone before. She feels about all
of us exactly as I feel about her; she's known us all too long and well,
and she sees only our unappealing qualities by now.

We had dinner first, and then afterwards we danced. We played records
on the phonograph and danced to them: "Kalua," which was just going
out, and "April Showers," which was just coming in, and others which
were in between.[20] The phonographs of the day were upright consoles,
generically called victrolas, although other manufacturers in addition
to the Victor Company marketed them. The average one still had to
be cranked by hand, although a few of the costlier ones could now be
operated on electrical current, but that was as far as mechanization had
gone. They stopped after just one record each time, and a new one had
to be put on by hand. We were uncomplaining, though. Our older brothers
and sisters, or at least the younger ones among our parents, had had
to rely for the most part on player pianos and hand-played pianos, and
squeaky, open-topped little turntables with tremendous tulip-horn
amplifiers, when they wanted to dance in their homes.

We had dinner and we danced, and that's all there really was to
the party.

We were the last ones to leave, Vera and I. I think we would have
stayed on even longer if it weren't for the fact that we were now reduced
(from my point of view, at least) to being alone with the unpleasing
Janet. Vera seemed not to mind how long we stayed. She was so keyed
up and animated from the hours-long peak of stimulation whipped up

by the party (just like an actress is after an opening night, I suppose) that she kept talking away without a let-up, as if there were still dozens of people there and not just three of us.

Janet, whom I had frequently known to be quite ungracious and even blunt in her dismissals (she had once said to a whole group of us, holding the door back at full width, "All right, everybody out; go home now"), seemed to enjoy having her stay. She sat beside Vera, an arm about her shoulder, nibbling at something from the refreshment table, drinking in everything she said with little nods and grins of accord. But it was close to one o'clock, which was still a fairly raffish hour for us at that stage of our lives, and I finally suggested to Vera she'd better let me take her home.

"Oh, what a lovely party that was!" she burst out as we emerged from the glowingly warm building into the cold, bracing night air, which immediately formed little wisps of steamy breath in front of our faces. "I never dreamed I'd have such a good time. My head's still swimming from it." And while I was busy scanning the street for a cab, she spread her coat and dress out wide between her outstretched hands and executed a succession of little whirling dance steps, waltz-turns, there on the sidewalk, turning, reversing, then turning back again.

Back at her house, we hustled all the way up those six flights of stairs, and then stopped suddenly almost at the top, and threw our arms around each other, as much in high spirits as in love. We stood there, and we kissed, and we whispered so low that no one standing right beside us could have heard, even if there had been someone standing right beside us.

Something more could have happened; she would not have opposed it. She was stirred by the party, intoxicated by her success at it, and this would have been part of that, and that would have been part of this. There is an unspoken understanding, a wordless language, at certain times, and even a youngster such as I was then, can sense and translate it. The half turn her head made against my shoulder, lying inert, passive, submissive, the way her hand dropped off my arm and hung down loose, the play of her breath as soft as the ebb and flow of breath-mist on a mirror, against my face, were words enough, no real ones were needed. This is part of the race's instinct.

But I didn't want it to happen. I did, but I didn't. And I made the didn't master the did. She had me accustomed now, conditioned now. I wanted her this way, the way she was, the way she had been on the bench that night. I had this image of her. I wanted to keep it, I didn't want to take anything away from it. (I didn't realize until years later that that's all there are, are our images of things. There are no realities. There are only the hundred different approximations of reality that are our images of it, no two the same, from man to man, from case to case, from place to place.)

There was a breathless springtime charm about her this way, a fragile sway she exerted over me, which would have been gone at a touch. Maybe a more heated, more grown love would have taken its place. But only for a while. Then that would have gone too, as it always does in such cases. And nothing would have been left. Not the first, not the second.

It wasn't a mere matter of purity or non-purity. Even that young, I wasn't narrow-minded. That was a mere cuticle-distinction.

It was partly possessive: you have something that belongs to you, that you value, like a bright new necktie or a leather wallet or a chrome lighter with your initials on it, and you don't want to get a stain on it, you don't want to deface it.

There was part self-esteem in it, I think. Your girl had to be better than any other girl around, or what was the use of her *being* your girl? You were so good yourself that you rated only the best, nothing less would do. Caesar's sweetheart.

But it was idealistic, mostly. If you're not going to be idealistic at that age, you're never going to be idealistic at all.

I don't know. I didn't know then, I still don't now. Who can explain the heart, the mind, the things they make you do?

I dropped one foot down to the step below, and took my arms off her.

"You better get inside, Vera." I said. "You better say goodnight to me."

And then I said again, "You better hurry up and get inside, Vera."

"Aren't you going to kiss me goodnight first?" she said softly.

"No, say it from up there. Not down here."

She went up the three or four remaining steps to the level, and took her key out and opened the door with it. Then she turned and looked at me as she went in. I saw her put the backs of a couple of her fingers across her lips; then she tipped them toward me in a secretive kissing sign. Still looking at me to the last, she slowly drew the door closed past her face, very slowly and very softly, almost without a sound.

She didn't come to the bench the next afternoon. I waited there for her for several hours, with that slowly fading afterglow you're left with on the day after a party, wanting to share it with her by talking the whole thing over, but she didn't come. Finally, when the early winter twilight had closed down and turned the whole world into a sooty, charcoal line drawing, all of black and gray, I got up and left, knowing she wasn't coming any more this late, and knowing just as surely I'd see her the following day. I didn't even stop by her house to find out what had kept her away, because I felt sure it was nothing more than a case of her being over tired from the night before, and of having slept late as a result.

But the next day she didn't come again either, and I wondered about it. I wondered if she'd stayed out too late with me to suit her family, and they were keeping her away from me for a few days to show their disapproval. But they hadn't been home yet themselves, to all appearances, when I'd brought her back.

Then I wondered if something had happened at the party that had offended or displeased her, something that she hadn't told me about. But I remembered how she'd danced in exuberance out on the sidewalk after we'd left, so it didn't seem likely it was that.

The third time she disappointed me, it was already the start of a new week, the party was already three or four days in back of us now, and I didn't wait any longer. The only possible explanation left was that she'd been taken ill; she might have caught cold that night, she'd been thinly dressed and it had been stingingly cold from what I remembered. And if she was ill, I wanted her at least to know I'd asked for her, and not let her think I'd been completely indifferent. So after a forlorn half hour's token vigil on the bench, with no real anticipation even at the start, I got up again and went over to her house to see if I could find out anything.

I don't recall any longer whether I made two visits over there on two successive days, on the first of which I merely loitered about in front of the place, in hopes either of catching sight of her or else of questioning somebody who might possibly know her (such as the little girl who had carried her message the night of the party), and on the second of which I finally went all the way up the stairs as far as her door; or whether the two telescoped themselves into one and the same occasion. But I do know that, all else having failed, I finally stood at the top of the six flights of stairs and I finally knocked at her door.

After a moment's wait I heard a single heavy crunch of the flooring just on the other side of it; I imagine the one board that had been trodden on creaked, while all the rest of them did not.

A voice asked: "Who's that?" A woman's, but that was all I recognized about it.

"Me," I said. "Vera's friend, Con." (To my own ears, it sounded like a faltering quaver that came out of me.)

The door opened, and her mother stood there.

Her face wasn't friendly. I couldn't decipher exactly what was on it at first, but it was set in bleak, grim lines and no smile broke on it.

"And is it Vera you're asking after?" she said, and I can still remember the thick Irish twist of speech she gave it.

I nodded and swallowed a lump of self-consciousness in my throat.

Her voice grew louder and warmer, but not the warmth of congeniality, the warmth of glittering, spark-flying resentment. "You have the nerve to come here and ask for her? You have the nerve to come here to this door? *You?*"

She kept getting louder by the minute.

"I should think you'd have the decency to stay home, and not show your face around here. Isn't it enough you've done? Well, isn't it?" And she clamped her hands to the sides of her head, as when you're trying to stifle some terrible recollection.

I drew back a step, stunned, congealed with consternation. Only one explanation was able to cross my mind. I knew nothing had happened on the stairs that night. But maybe they didn't, maybe they thought something had. And if they did, what way was there I could ever—

"Now go on about your business!" she said sternly. The expression "Get lost" had not yet come into general parlance, but she used an approximation of it. "Take yourself off," I think it was.

By that time I was partly down the stairs already, and then had stopped again and half-turned around to her to hear the rest of it out.

"Stay away from here. There's no Vera here for you."

The door gave a cataclysmic bang, and that was the end of it. There was no Vera there for me.

I have often wondered since why it was such a long time after that before I ran into Frankie again. Maybe it actually wasn't, but it seemed so at the time. Weeks, if not quite months. But our paths didn't happen to cross, I guess, for we each had differing interests by now. The hero-worship stage was long a thing of the past. I had probably grown out of it by myself; I don't think my friendship with Vera had anything to do with ending it. And I hadn't sought him out, because it had never occurred to me that he might be in a better position than I to pick up the neighborhood rumors and gossip, his ear being closer attuned to it than mine, in a way.

Anyway, one day we came along on opposite sides of the same street, he going one way, I the other. He threw up his arm to me, I flung up mine to him, and he crossed over to me. Or we met in the middle, whichever it was.

We made a couple of general remarks, mostly about his current boxing activities (he was still in the amateur category, he told me, but about ready to become pro; all he needed was to find the right manager). Then he suddenly said: "That was tough about your friend, wasn't it?"

I must have sensed something serious was about to come up; I quickly became alerted, even before the conversation had gotten any further. "Vera? What was tough? What was?" I asked tautly.

"About her getting caught up with like that."

"Caught up with how?" I insisted.

"What are you, serious?" he said impatiently. "I thought you knew about it. The whole block knows. How come you don't know about it, when you been going around with her so much lately? Practically steady."

"All of a sudden I didn't see her any more," I tried to explain. "She dropped out of sight, and I couldn't find out why. Nobody told me."

"I could'a' told you," he said. "Why di'ntya come to me?"

"Well, what is it?" I urged. "What?"

"She was picked up," he said flatly.

I didn't understand at first; I thought he meant a flirtatious pick-up, by some stranger on the street.

"Picked up by some fellow? She wasn't that kind. I know her too well."

"I don't mean picked up by some fellow. Picked up by the cops. She was taken in."

I felt as though one of his best punches had hit me squarely between the eyes. All I could see for a minute were swirls in front of them. Like a pair of those disks with alternate black and white circular lines that keep spinning into a common center, but they never come to an end, they always keep right on coming.

"For what?" I managed to get out when they'd finally thinned somewhat and started to fade away. "What for?"

I guess he could see by my face the kind of effect he had had on me; it seemed to make him feel regretful that he'd told me. "Don't take it like that," he said contritely. "I wounna told you, if I knew it was going to get you like that."

"But why?" was all I kept saying, tearful without any tears, querulous, resentful, all those things at once. "What'd she *do*? They can't just come along like that and haul anybody in they want to."

He didn't stop to argue that with me; evidently he felt the facts did it for him. "You know the old lady she worked for part-time, the rich old lady on West End Avenue—? She ever tell you about her?"

"Yeah, I knew she worked for her," I said marginally.

"The old lady put in a complaint about her to the cops. She called them up and told them there was an expensive fur coat missing out of her closet, and she accused Vera of swiping it. So they went over there to Vera's place, looking for it, at eight o'clock in the morning. She was still in bed, but they found it folded up underneath her mattress."

"She had one she was paying for on time—" I tried to say in her defense.

"Na," he said juridically. "The old lady identified it, it had the same labels on it."

"Then what'd they do?" I faltered, sickish in the throat with backed-up salty fluid.

"They made her get dressed, and they took her with them. She claimed she just borrowed it to wear for one night, and was going to bring it right back the next day. The trouble was she couldn't prove that, because they caught up with her too quick and she still had it in the room with her when they got there."

An excruciating little mental image crossed my mind, of her coming out the street-doorway of her house, that same doorway where she hadn't wanted the neighbors to see her "all dressed up," but now with two men alongside her, people looking on from windows and from the steps, holding her head down, and with tears probably, tears almost certainly, gliding down her shame-flushed face.

"But if the old lady got her coat back, why didn't she just let her go?" I wailed querulously.

"She wanted to teach her a lesson, I guess. She said she'd been very good to Vera, and Vera had repaid her by stealing from her behind her back." And he interpolated sagely: "You know, them old ladies can be very mean sometimes, especially when it comes to losing something like a fur coat."

"I know," I assented mournfully. To both of us, I suppose, a woman of forty would have been what we considered an old lady.

"She was sore, and she wouldn't drop the charges. They brung Vera up before a magistrate—I doanno if it was in juvenile court or where, but I guess it was there, because she's still a minor—and he committed her to a reformatory for six months.[21] She's up there now, at some farm they got upstate."

And he added, quite unnecessarily, "That's why you haven't seen her around any more."

After a wordless pause of several moments, I started to move away from him.

"Hey, come back here," he said. "Come back here." He was trying to be sympathetic, consolatory, in a gruff sort of way, which was the only way he knew how.

I kept on going, drifting away from him.

Then he tried to come after me and rejoin me. I didn't see him because I didn't turn to look, but I knew he was, because I could tell by the sound of his feet, coming along behind me. I motioned to him with a backward pass of my hand to leave me alone, to go on off.

I didn't want him to see my face.

I felt like a dog that's just had its paw stepped on real hard, and it goes limping off on three feet and is leery of everyone, doesn't want anyone to come near it for awhile. The only thing I didn't do was whimper like one.

All the winter long I'd pass there now and then, and every time I passed I'd seem to see her standing there in the doorway. Just the way I'd seen her standing sometimes when we'd met by her door instead of at the park bench.

Complete; intact in every detail: looping her tamoshanter around by its headband on the point of one finger. Much more than an illusion; a life-size cut-out, like those figures they sometimes stood up outside of theatres. So real that the checks of her coat hid the grubby brownstone doorway-facing behind where they were. So real that even the remembered position of her feet repeated itself on the brownstone doorstep, and they seemed to be standing there once again just as they once had: one planted flat out a little way before her so that the shank of her leg curved gracefully outward a little to reach it; the other bent backward behind her, and planted vertically against the sideward part of the doorway. And as I'd once noticed, when she thrust a door closed behind her with a little kick-back of her heel, here again she gave grace, not grotesqueness, to this odd little posture.

But then as I'd look and look, and look some more, longingly (not so much with love—for what did I know of love at nineteen? Or for that matter, what did I know of it at thirty-nine or forty-nine or fifty-nine?—as with some sense of isolation, of pinpointed and transfixed helplessness under the stars, of being left alone, unheard and unaided to face some final fated darkness and engulfment slowly advancing across the years toward me, that has hung over me all my life), the brownstone-facing would slowly peer back through the checks of her coat, the doorstep would be empty of her disparately placed feet, and I'd have to go on my way alone again. As all of us have to go alone, anywhere that we go, at any time and at any place.

The young, I think, feel loneliness far more acutely than the older do, for they have expected too much, they have expected everything. Those older never expect quite everything, or more than just a little at best, and when loneliness strikes, their lack of complete expectation in the first place dulls the sharp edge of it somewhat.

The spring came again, and then that warmed itself into early summer, and by now it was a year since I had first met her. I still thought of her very often, but I no longer thought of her all the time. Her immediacy had faded.

One night in June I was passing along Eighth Avenue again, and as the corner of One Hundred and Fourteenth Street came abreast of me and opened up the side-street into view, it suddenly seemed to blaze up from one end to the other like a rippling straw-fire, an illusion produced by scores of light bulbs strung criss-cross from one side of the street to the other, and fidgeting in the slight breeze. Vehicular entry had been blocked off by a wooden traffic horse placed at the street entrance. People were banked on both sidewalks looking on, and between them, out in the middle, tightly packed couples were dancing. They were holding a block party on the street.

Block parties were nothing new. In fact, by this time they were already well on their way out. They had first originated about four years before, at the time of the mass demobilization, when each individual block celebrated the return to its midst of those young men who had seen service overseas by holding a community homecoming party in their honor out in the street (because that was the only place that could conveniently accommodate all the participants).

But this was the early summer of 1923, not 1919 any longer; the last soldiers had finished coming back long ago; the only ones left were regulars, on garrison duty along the Rhine, at the Koblenz bridgehead. Another thing: the climate of public opinion had noticeably changed in the meantime. The naive fervor of the first postwar year or two had now given place to that cynicism toward all things military and patriotic that characterized the remainder of the decade. So the occasion for this particular party must have been something else: a church benefit or charity affair of some kind.

I moved in among the onlookers and stood there with my shoes tipping over the edge of the curb, watching. The music wasn't very good, but it was enthusiastic and noisy, and that was the mood the crowd was in, so that was all that mattered. They were probably amateurs who lived on the block themselves, and each one had brought his particular instrument down into the street with him, and joined forces with the others. But they were so uneven they were almost good, because the music of the moment was supposed to be played in just that sort of jagged, uneven time, anyway. I can still remember them blaring and blatting away at two of the current favorites: "Dearest, You're the Nearest to my Heart" and "Down, Down Among the Sleepy Hills of Ten, Ten, Tennessee."[22]

Then as I stood there on the lip of the curbing, taking it all in, she was suddenly there in front of me. I never knew afterward which direction she'd come from, because I didn't have time to see. She was just suddenly there, that was all, and I was looking at Vera again.

She hadn't changed much. The even-all-around cut might have been missing from her hair, but I can't be sure, for I didn't look up at it, just looked at her. She had on a fresh, summery little dress, orchid in color, that much I seem to remember. It was both gauzy and crisp at the same time, most likely what they call organdy.

But there was one thing I did notice clearly, as we looked straight into one another's eyes, one thing that hadn't been there before. There was a little diagonal crevice, like a nick or slit, traced downward from the inside corner of each eye, slanted like an accent mark and just as brief as one. It couldn't have been called a crease, for she was too young to have creases yet. It wasn't a furrow either, it wasn't deep enough for that.

Studying her, I wondered what had caused it. Tear-tracks, maybe, from excessive crying? No, not tears alone. Tears maybe, but something else as well. Long, sleepless nights of brooding, of frustration and rebellion.

If they grew longer, deeper, I sensed somehow they would change the expression of her face, give her eyes a hardened, crafty aspect. But it was too soon to do that yet. All they were so far was a mark of hurt; they gave her eyes an apprehensive, reproachful look.

I don't know what we said first. Probably I said her name, and she said mine.

Then she moved her mouth upward toward me a little, and we kissed.

"It's been an awful long time I last saw you," I said, skipping the "since" in the hurry of my speech. Tactless, without meaning to be. But what else could I have said? I hadn't seen her just yesterday.

"I've been away," she said reticently.

I wondered if she knew I knew. I hoped she didn't. I would have liked to tell her that I didn't know, but I couldn't figure out a way that wouldn't tell her that I did know.

"Working," she added even more reticently.

"You still live here on the block?" I asked her.

She answered that with less constraint. "Not any more," she said. "I just came around tonight to see what the old neighborhood looked like."

Then, as if to break the chain-continuity of questions, she suddenly suggested: "Dance with me. It's too hard to try to talk with all that noise they're making."

I stepped down to the asphalt roadbed she was standing on, which had been powdered over with something to make it less abrasive to the dancers' feet.

We moved a few steps, a few steps only, and then even that was taken away from me.

A girl came jostling and thrusting her way through the mangle of dancers, someone I had never seen before. She touched Vera on the back or something, I couldn't see what it was, to attract her attention.

"What're you doing?" she demanded in a tone of urgency. "Don't you know they're waiting for us?"

"I just met an old friend," Vera told her happily, and she indicated me with her head, about to introduce us.

The other girl brushed that aside, as if to say: This is no time for that now. She didn't even look toward me.

"This is the second time they've sent me out to look for you," she went on rebukingly. "How much longer you going to be? You must have seen everything you wanted to by now. What's there to see around here, anyway? They won't like it if you keep them waiting much longer."

"All right, I'm coming," Vera said with a sort of passivity, as though she were used to being told what to do.

"I guess I have to go now," she said, turning to me, with a regretful little smile that, whether she meant it or not, was a pleasant balm to my feelings.

She turned aside from my still-upheld arms and followed the other girl back through the crowd. And after a moment, I went after the two of them, more slowly.

Once up on the sidewalk and in the clear, they broke into a choppy little quick-step that girls sometimes use, not quite a run but more than a walk, Vera still a trifle in back of the other one.

"But when am I going to see you again?" I called out after her, bewildered by the rapidity with which I'd found her, only to lose her again.

She turned her head around, but without breaking stride in the little jogging trot she was engaged in, and called back reassuringly: "Real soon, Con. And that's a promise."

Then they both made the turn of the corner and whisked from sight.

I went down there after them, not to try to stop them, for I knew that wouldn't have worked, but simply to see if I could get a look at who it was they were hurrying so to join.

As I put my head around the corner, a pale-stockinged after-leg was drawing from sight into a car that was standing there, and then the car door cracked shut with that flat sound they always have.

It was standing, oh I don't know, about ten yards along from the corner, and there were a number of men in it, exactly how many I couldn't tell, maybe three, possibly four, but certainly more than just two to pair off with the girls. They were older men, not youths my own and Vera's age. This was more a matter of outline than anything else, since I couldn't see their faces to the slightest degree, but the impression of maturity was unmistakable. The massiveness of their shoulders gave it to me, and the breadth of the backs of their necks, and they were all alike wearing rather too dressy snap-brim felt hats (and this was already June). One of them was smoking a cigar, I saw it glow for a moment in the darkness under the roof of the car, and the livid concentric swirl it made was much larger than a mere cigarette ember would have been, particularly if seen from a distance like that.

And finally, the car itself was not of a type that young men would have owned or cared to own or habitually been found driving around in. It was no runabout or roadster or rattling, motto-inscribed "flivver." It was a closed car, a black sedan, a very heavy-set, high-powered affair. It almost looked custom-made. It had more than the usual amount of burnished hardware on the outside (door handles, headlights, and a smaller, cone-shaped swivel light up alongside the windshield). If it weren't for the wheels, it could have resembled a coffin.

I don't know who or what they were, and I never will. Maybe they were just hard-bitten older men, older than the two girls with them, toughened up by years of wresting every hard-fought buck from a reluctant world. Without grace, without compunction, without laughter. Harmless otherwise in general (except of course to young girls such as those). Non-lethal, or I should say, non-illicit.

And then again maybe not. About two or three years after that, around '25 or '26, when an awareness of the new type of public violence, which the First War and Prohibition had bred between them, finally percolated through to the public consciousness from the specialized areas to which it had been confined until now—the police-files, crime- and police-reporters, certain politicians, speakeasy operators, and the like—and new words like *gangster* and *racketeer* and *public enemy* began to sprinkle the pages of the newspapers more and more often, along with accounts of nocturnal ambuscades and machine-gun fusillades and murders in garages and warehouses and concrete-weighted drownings along the water's edge...Every time I'd come across one of them, something brought back the picture of that car to my mind's eye.

And I'd wonder then, as I still wonder now, was it men of that kind she and her friend had gone off with that night? Some of their earlier prototypes, their very first vanguard? Or was there just a superficial resemblance there that fooled my untrained, unknowledgeable eye?

And I'd hope, every time I thought about it, that that was what it was, and nothing more.

But I never could be sure.

It didn't even have a tail-light on, to follow its recession by. But like a great big inky patch against the paler night it grew smaller and smaller as it dwindled down the street, stealthily, without sound, until it had contracted into extinction and was there no more.

We never saw each other again, in this world, in this lifetime. Or if we did, we didn't know each other.

III
Even God Felt the Depression

"Even God Felt the Depression" is a vivid description of Woolrich's feverishly desperate attempt, in 1933, to compose another successful romantic novel. His only hope for an escape from Depression-era poverty seemed to be this: he could write a novel to be sold to Hollywood. After struggling with the new manuscript for weeks, Woolrich finally feels a renewed sense of hope, and he looks forward to a kind of salvation. Awaiting his agent's verdict, he stops to pray before a Roman Catholic icon in a church he passes while walking to the subway stop.

While the reader awaits an answer to Woolrich's prayer, a mood of despair gradually overwhelms the prose, until it is as black as his suspense fiction. At the end of the story comes a startling fatalistic gesture, and an unexpected irony. This episode reveals how it came to be that, as surely as if he had been murdered, Woolrich one day lost all faith in God. Perhaps it explains his move from romantic to suspense fiction too.

I'd hardly made a cent that whole year. Or for that matter the one before, or the one before that. The Depression had become stabilized by this time. It was now accepted as a permanent condition. The sharp downgrade had come to an end, and it had leveled off, but with that had also ended all the earlier hopes of an upturn, of a magic-wand dismissal, of a just-around-the-corner mirage of a picture-postcard goddess called Prosperity spilling roses and gold pieces indiscriminately out of a brimming cornucopia. People had given up hoping. It was now a part of everyday existence, and everyday existence is the most difficult thing of all to change; all the emperors, kings and conquerors have found that out. It was the Present, it was the Thirties, you couldn't have one without the other. Even the songs were tinged with it. "Brother, Can You Spare a Dime?"; "I'll never be the same, Stars have lost their meaning for me—"; "No more money in the bank—"; "Potatoes are cheaper, tomatoes are cheaper—."[1] For the first time, love, in this context, ran a poor second.

As the new decade plodded dejectedly on, holding an apple for sale in one hand, an upturned hat in the other, it became hard even to remember the time when there hadn't been a depression. That time was legend, not reality any more. There'd been a time when there'd been Indians and colonists. There'd been a time when the States warred against each other.

So too had there been a time when you went to parties and speakeasies. And the only thing that mattered, if you were a girl then, was to wear the shortest possible haircut and the shortest possible skirts. And if you were a young man, to know the greatest number of speakeasies so long and so well that you were called by your first name there and admitted on sight when the small grille first opened and an eye looked out at you, without having to present one of those meaningless, ubiquitous little cards that seemed to be floating around by the thousands and say, "Charlie sent me," or "John," or "Joe"; only the uninitiated had to do that any longer, by the time the period reached its crest. That was for visitors, out-of-towners, strangers, and even they were seldom refused. Even a policeman would now and then drop in, not for purposes of inspection—for he was on their payroll, so to speak—but to have a friendly drink; and on one occasion at least, at which I was present, to sing "Silver Threads Among the Gold" in a beautiful baritone for the entertainment of the other customers, who then passed around the hat.[2]

During the Twenties, there was always money around somewhere near at hand, somehow. If not right in your pocket, then over in your room, or your apartment. If not in your apartment, then around at the bank. If not around at the bank, then in some friend's pocket, until there was once more some around at the bank. Never a matter of more than a few days or a week at the most.

Of course it didn't just grow on trees, no. You worked for it. But the work was so easy and the pay was so large. And the working part of the day seemed so short and inconsequential compared to the long, delectable speakeasy nights and dawnings. And if you were dissatisfied with the work (and it was the worker who was dissatisfied more often than those he worked for) you simply went on to another place where the pay was even larger. Only absolute ineptitude or a personal feud with a superior seemed able to cost anyone his job against his own volition. And if you were a writer, or at least an entertainment-writer, such as I had started out to be, you shared in this general run of things. The work was easy and the pay was large.

Those were marvelous times. Not even the time before the French Revolution equaled them in splurge and squander: for then the poor had been discontented. Now there were no poor at all. (Until the bottom fell out of the whole world, and everyone was poor together.)

But all that was long ago, dimmed by the mists of time. Those days had been whisked backwards out of the memory as though they had been forty years before and not just four.

And now, it was no time in which to be a writer. Food and shelter were the essentials. They could no longer be just taken for granted, they had to be struggled for now. And thousands had even lost them altogether. Whole families had broken up. The wives and children, because women are less fit for a nomadic life, went back under their parents' roofs, if they were lucky enough to have parents who still had roofs. To live it out somehow, to bide their time, until the dreadful thing should pass, if it ever did pass. The men built colonies of shacks, of cartons and of packing cases and gasoline drums and whatever they could get their hands on, and drew their drinking water from the nearest comfort station (because they could be sure at least it was sterile there) and got their food standing in endless, dejected lines outside of public soup kitchens and other charitable hand-out places.

These shacks along the river banks, and whatever other public unrestricted ground they were allowed to trespass upon, were commonly called Hoovervilles, in unjust deprecation of the man who had not at all caused the situation but simply inherited it.[3]

No, it was no time in which to be a writer. Magazines were expiring all over, dropping off like autumn leaves falling from trees. Who had time for books, for magazines? Who had the money to waste on fairy tales of a world that had vanished? The two great mutually antipathetic forces in this life have never been love and death, but love and hunger. Whichever gains the ascendancy, the other suffers by it.

No one cared who got the girl in the story anymore. They knew he couldn't keep her very long, nowadays.

On the other hand, the new times were too new to be written about yet. Those who would write about them a little later on were still busy living them now.

I had given my situation as a writer in these indigent times much thought. I had had to. There was no money coming in anymore, absolutely not a single penny. My last sale had been late in 1932, already nearly half a year back by this time (counting from the check and not the acceptance date, which were not the same thing by any means), to a magazine called *Illustrated Love Stories*, which had had the great advantage, if nothing else, of being displayed and sold throughout the widespread and popular Woolworth Five-and-Ten Cent Store chain.[4] But even that money by now had fallen by the wayside and was no more.

At the time of the memorable bank closure of February 1933 I had had exactly sixty-one dollars to my name in one of the locked-up banks. This amount I can stake my word on, because I distinctly recall a friend of mine saying he envied me having even that much, as he himself had had only sixteen left in, and then we both noticed that the figures were reversible, that is, interchangeable if turned around. When the banks reopened I quickly took the sixty-one out, mainly because I'd already pledged a good part of it toward my daily needs, and the remainder because I was apprehensive, as many others were, that the banks might reclose again any day as unexpectedly as they had the first time, and I wanted the few dollars out in the open where I could put my hands on them.

By now, about two months later, this sixty-one dollars was all gone, but I'd found various ways of tiding myself over in the interim. There was a beautiful gold watch my father's younger brother had left me. This was constructed in such a way that I managed to live off it for some time, in the way that you eat an artichoke, leaf by leaf. It had two thick outer casings, one on each side, and then two somewhat thinner ones inside, making four altogether. All of the finest purest gold. Its works were heavily jeweled, and then a massive gold fob went with it, such as they had worn in those days.

At intervals which I spaced as widely as I could, I used to take it downtown, near the foot of Wall Street, over toward the river, to an assay office that bought precious metals, and have them carefully pry off one lid, so that the rest wouldn't be damaged, and have that weighed and sell it to them. I got surprisingly liberal amounts each time, too; when the Nineties made something of gold, they weren't stingy with the gold. Still, I felt bad each time I had to part with some more of it—nostalgic, wistful, penitent—and surprisingly, considering that it was the gift of a man whom I hadn't seen since my early boyhood.

When the last of it was all gone finally, and only a scrap of black grosgrain ribbon was left to show what it had been, I started in on my books and sold them piecemeal as well. I had a considerable number of limited editions given to me as gifts at Christmastime by the publishers themselves, during the course of the years, all numbered, inscribed, rag-papered, gilt-edged and beautifully bound.

I used to get a miserable couple of dollars for one of them each time: for a thing which could not have been obtained on the open market at any price. I had a little red-and-black tiered bookcase in my room, and the increasing gaps in its various compartments used to stare out at me accusingly, like wide-open eyes, and I'd want to turn my head away.

Then one night, right after I'd parted with a costly deluxe edition of the Life of Isadora Duncan, I happened to go by a bar.[5] It was one of those bland, springlike evenings that always seemed to stir a longing for recreation even more than at other times. The lights looked inviting, and there was the pulse-beat of music coming from inside. So I went in, and bought a beer, and stood there with it for awhile.

Then just as I was about to order a second one, the thought suddenly came to me: This is someone's life you're drinking down. Her glories and her triumphs, her aspirations and her strivings, her heartaches and her happiness. Should this be the end result of all that? Is this all she lived for? Is this all the transmutation her life deserves? Cheap rank-smelling beer going down some brash young guy's gullet? And afterward maybe, in some foul washroom, to turn into something even worse.

How would you like it if, someday after you're gone, and have left behind you (if you do) just one worthwhile book, one thing you put everything into, one thing to live on after you, one thing to show you'd ever been around in the first place; then how would you like it if some young fellow who never had heard of you, and wouldn't have cared if he had, stood up one night and did that to your life's work?

I winced, and put down my glass, and got out of there fast, and I never repeated that again. Not on the proceeds of anyone else's book, anyone else's lifeblood, at least.

But I was starved for recreation, and had to get it the best way I could, even if I had no money to pay for it.

There was a rooftop motion picture theatre nearby at that time called Japanese Gardens (most likely because its overhead aisle-lights were encased in a few pseudo-Japanese lanterns; there was never anything else Japanese that I could notice about it).[6] It was not an open-air theatre, but simply a roofed over one on the top floor of the building. The great advantage of the place was this: If you bought an admission and entered legitimately, so to speak, which I could not do because I couldn't afford the twenty-five cents, you were carried from the street-level lobby by elevator up to the theatre itself. But in compliance with Fire Department regulations there was an enclosed safety-staircase that ran down from above and gave onto the street by means of a heavy metal door, which could not be opened from the outside, but could easily be pushed aside from the inside. The elevator was slow in coming up, and very often people who had finished seeing the show and wanted to leave were too impatient to wait for it and would come down the stairs instead. I used to hang around the outside of this staircase door and watch it like a hawk, and when I saw it start to swing open, I'd hook my hand to it and keep it akimbo until I could get in myself. Those leaving never offered any objection; they seemed tolerant that way. I didn't mind climbing up the five or six flights. It meant nothing to me; I considered it well worthwhile. They changed the bill twice a week, and for several weeks I took in each new show and managed to see a fair sampling of the best feature pictures of the early Thirties.

But one night, careless from long immunity, I timed myself wrong, and the usher on duty must have spotted me without my knowing it, as I crossed the vulnerable open space between the stairhead and the last row of seats. He waited until I'd picked out a nice comfortable aisle seat, then I felt a rock-hard tap on my shoulder, and when I looked up, he grimly and wordlessly swung his thumb back and forth a few times toward the staircase.

He didn't actually take hold of my arm, but he insisted on escorting me all the way down the stairs again to where I had originally entered. The sound of his slapping footsteps counterpointing mine down five or six whole flights irritated me for some reason.

"All right," I protested, offended. "I'm going. You don't have to come all the way down to the bottom with me."

He came back at me with a catch-phrase popular at the time: "You're telling *me* you're going? No, I'm telling *you!*"

When we were both on the outside, he securely reclosed the front door from that side and then he himself reentered by the front way, in order to be able to ride the elevator up, leaving me standing by myself on the dismal sidewalk, heaving and as cracklingly indignant as though I had been unjustly put upon.

And this was the way things had been going with me right then. It was, as I said at the beginning, no time in which to be a writer.

But I knew I had to be. It was something I couldn't help being. It was something that had been in me all my life, from the time that I was a kid and first kept a schoolboyish diary. It was something that I couldn't push aside until later, when I would know the real meaning of unhappiness, not these little trials and tribulations I knew now. I used to round my fist, and swing it with all my might into my other palm, whenever I received a disappointment or a rejection, and mutter doggedly: "I'll beat this game yet! I'll beat it yet!"

I thought about it, and thought about it, and finally I came to a decision. There was one solution and only one. There was one way to make enough money all at one time to tide me over, take the curse off this hand-to-mouth existence I was leading, give me a start back onto my feet at least. Books wouldn't do it, they weren't selling. Magazines wouldn't do it, they weren't buying.

But there was one medium of profit left. The motion-picture industry. Although its earnings, too, had gone down greatly, it was so worldwide, so universal, had become such a standby of modern-day living, that it alone managed to keep its head well above the general inundation. Many a man without work or hope of work (or after awhile even the desire for it) managed somehow to find a stray quarter and go into some small moviehouse at noon when it opened, and spend the rest of the day in there trying to forget that he had no work or hope of work. Smoking, eating a stale roll, watching the anesthetic up on the screen.

The motion-picture industry still bought from writers. It needed them, it fed upon them, they were its fodder. And when it bought, it still paid, not by the hundreds of dollars but by the thousands.

The problem, though, was to offer them something that stood a good chance of acceptance, that was likely to be bought. To come up with anything else would be just a waste of time. All the things I had on hand, already done, were as stale as the speakeasies and the knee-length skirts; I knew no one would touch them.

Then when I least expected it I came across, quite by accident, something that seemed to have just the right possibilities. Opening my valise one day to scramble through it for something (it always made me wistful to bring it out into the open and see the travel- and hotel-stickers still all over it—"Red Star Line," "Holland-America Line," "Hotel Colón, Barcelona," "Pension Isabella, Muenchen"—from the carefree days now gone), I upturned the first few pages of a novel I had started in Paris two years before and never gone ahead with.[7]

It was called *I Love You, Paris,* a title which would have been invalidated a couple of decades later by the hit song from *Can Can.*[8] There was very little of it done, just an opening chapter, but I found when I reread it that what I had intended to do with it was still fresh enough in my mind, and in any case there was a key-sheet along with it, with a skeleton plot-framework outlined on it.[9]

My volatile optimism (at least where my own material was concerned) immediately blazed up on reading it over, and it seemed to me to be the very thing I was looking for, the best possible bet for what I had in mind. For one thing, the period I had picked for it—pre-war Paris, 1912—was still completely untouched as far as the pictures were concerned, and I felt that should make a very good selling point. The screen was known to be always on the lookout for new, unhackneyed settings for its stories.

My protagonists were a pair of professional ballroom dancers, the man much older than the girl, his pupil and protégé, one of a long succession he has had throughout his career, whom he has taught to dance, made famous, and who then have repaid him by leaving him for some other, younger man. He is in love with his current partner, but she looks upon him only as a father and mentor.

Along comes a younger man the girl's own age, and he and she fall in love. Then the young people have a misunderstanding and fall out again. She disappears, and he goes looking for her everywhere and cannot find her. Then, on her opening night, the night of her professional debut, he happens to pass the place where she is to appear and recognizes her from a photograph in the foyer. He goes in to watch her, thinking this will be the last time he will ever see her.

She has an enormous and dazzling success, and instantly becomes the sensation of Paris. But she has recognized him sitting out front, and immediately after the performance she runs out to him, throws her success over her shoulder, and they go off together.

Her partner, who has really got a bad deal out of the whole thing, accepts it with graceful resignation (he is used to it by now) and goes back to his former partner, who has been intermittently sending off sparks of jealousy in the background throughout the story. The implication is that they will continue to bicker like cat and dog, as they did the first time, but at least will understand each other.

There were also a couple of subplots to help fill the thing out, in a more or less comic vein. A rich fat maharajah becomes enamored of the girl, though he already has a retinue of vivacious young Parisiennes who follow him around all over, and a middle-aged American lady tourist from the Middle West, also well-to-do and speaking hilarious (I hoped) broken French, mistakes the young man for a gigolo and pursues him almost to distraction.

If all this sounds pretty bad, all I can say is it was. But we are always so much wiser in retrospect, all of us. I would have died to defend its merits then. At least it was no worse than anything else that was to be seen on the screen those days.

The format in which to present it had to be considered. I decided that a shortcut, simply to save myself work, wouldn't be advisable, would lessen its chances. That a synopsis or outline, what they called a short "treatment," wouldn't do any good. I felt it might be pigeonholed and forgotten, as they received literally thousands of such things. Moreover, to avoid later accusations of plagiarism, many of the studios, it was my understanding, refused to accept them, returning them unopened. Therefore, the only sensible thing to do would be to complete it first as a book, to write it out at full, toilsome length no matter how much labor was involved, to try to get it published by a book firm to start with, to give it that much more prestige, attract that much more attention to it, and then to immediately try to sell it from there, perhaps from the galley-proofs alone, without even waiting for formal publication.

This meant, and I knew it well, anywhere from six weeks to two months of the most driving, uninterrupted drudgery, amounting almost to self-immolation. To give up everything else, all thought of recreation. And to continue living in the meantime as I had been doing all the while: scraping along tooth and nail almost without any money to speak of, only nickels and dimes in my pocket. When you look back toward a certain age, two months isn't long. But when you *are* that certain age, two months is eternity.

It was a gamble, and a very great one. All or nothing. But I decided to take it. If I didn't try it, I still had nothing. But if I did try it, and I succeeded, then I had just about everything. The money problem would be over, for years to come. What other choice was there for me anyhow? I asked myself. I wasn't equipped for anything else. To wait on customers, sell things over a counter, either in a haberdashery or a grocery? There were thousands who could do it much better than I, and they couldn't get those jobs themselves, jobs like that weren't to be had. This was the only thing I knew how to do. So I tightened my belt, took a last regretful look at the corruscating, titillating world around me, and sat down and grimly bent to work.

As far as the book-publishing stage of it was concerned, that didn't worry me too much. I had a promising opening, or at least potential opening, waiting for me there. A man in the editorial field whom I'd dealt with in the past had, just shortly before this, been taken on at one of the smaller publishing houses—probably displacing somebody else, which was the only way it was done at this time. I'd known him in the halcyon days of four or five years before, and then lost track of him until now. I'll call him Irwin, since I've never been sure exactly what part he played in what happened later on, and have no wish even at this late date to do him an injustice. His own first name began with the same capital letter, at any rate.

I'd noticed a little squib about his new alignment in the book notes which the *Times* habitually ran on its daily book page, and I promptly got in touch with him and told him I'd started working on something.[10] He sounded very encouraging and hospitable, and urged me to let him see it as soon as I'd finished doing it. This of course might have been no more than the ordinary professional courtesy he would have extended to any published author, but I took a sanguine view of it.

There was of course no question of an advance before its completion, and I knew enough not to ask him for one, although it would have solved all my problems beautifully. If the thing was no good, I would have had no way of repaying it, and we both realized it. Publishers weren't using their money to speculate on anything sight unseen in those parlous days, except in the case of a big name, perhaps, and I was a writer of too dubious a stature to warrant it. I was fairly well known, but on the strength of fairly little accomplished. I wasn't by any means what could have been called a good risk at the time.

I had everything lined up now, and the rest was up to me. I worked, and I worked, and I worked. I worked in the morning, I worked in the afternoon, I worked at night. I don't think typewriter keys ever took such a hammering before. Perhaps stenographically, but never creatively.

The spring was advancing, and tantalizingly beautiful days came; there seemed to be an endless succession of them, as if purposely sent to plague me. New York may not be notable for its weather, but when it does turn out a fine day, no place else can top it. And just enough of that first delicate, immaculate green showed through its concrete crevices here and there to put nature's official seal on the season, adding a decorative touch, like the parsley on the omelette or the mint sprig in the lemonade. Each day had the effect on me of a champagne cocktail: golden and tingling and heady. And I couldn't even touch it, had to pass it by.

The nights were even more excruciating. To me those long lines of lights that flamed along the Avenues as far as the eye could see were never garish (as they probably were) but glamorous, seeming to hold out a promise of wonderment and magic, and I wanted to be out where they were. Everyone else was, in droves; I could see them passing the corner, from my window, in two continuous opposite-moving streams, and there I sat, in a solitary room, locked in the lonely pool of light cast by a desk lamp.

But I wouldn't leave the desk. I almost had to grab it with both hands and hang onto it for dear life, almost had to hook my ankles around its legs to stay on the chair, but I wouldn't leave it, no I wouldn't leave it. Consummation had to come first.

During this whole time I was having a great deal of difficulty with the hotel manager, Mr. Drew.[11] Difficulty avoiding him, I mean. I was chronically anywhere from a month to a month and a half behind in my room rent, and though I paid installments on it as often as I could, the gap was so great that I never could seem to bridge it and bring myself up to date. It was like a sort of hopeless treadmill. By the time I finished up one month, a new one would be over already.

Mr. Drew was a corpulent, apoplectic man and, in my case at least, a great believer in the personal appeal as far as rent-lag was concerned, always accompanied by numerous histrionic gestures such as clapping his forehead and flapping his hands about in a woebegone way. I suppose he had learned by now that all the standard methods, such as reminders from clerks, notations at the foot of bills, and even telephone calls, were of no avail in my case; they weren't, because there was nothing I could do to remedy the situation myself. He had come up through the ranks in the hotel business, starting first as a waiter, then maitre de, and so on, and I think basically we liked each other, but if we did, no two people who liked each other ever had such a scrappy, turbulent relationship as we.

The hotel had an elevator that used to continue on down below the lobby floor, where the desk was, and bring you out at the back of a drugstore that the building housed. From there you could gain the street, without having to pass the front desk and Mr. Drew's watchful eye.

I used this means of escape with great frequency until, as Drew became familiar with the tactic, its usefulness began to wane. For the elevator, unfortunately, had an old-fashioned lattice-work draw-gate securing it, which could be looked through, and when he would spot me in the interior of the car, trying to make myself as inconspicuous as possible as I continued on down below, he would dash out from around in back of the desk, chase down the entrance-steps, out the main entrance, and around the corner to the drugstore doorway, and I would walk right into his arms, so to speak, when I came quick-stepping out a minute later.

After several of these half-supplicating, half-stormy sidewalk fracases, I gave up coming out the side entrance, as an expedient that had outlived its usefulness. I couldn't give him his money, because I didn't have it to give in the first place, but I stopped trying to evade him, and he had to fall back on his original (and wholly unproductive) technique of bombarding me with countless bills, all with lurid crimson-ink "Past Due" stamps on them, and calling me in my room on the phone at varied hours of the day and night, ranging from eight in the morning until twelve midnight. He only stopped then because he went to bed around that hour himself, I suppose. I did more angrily severe banging up of the telephone receiver in those days than I have ever done in my life, before or since.

Thus we stalemated one another, and finally relapsed into a state of sullen, armed truce.

One night there was a knock at my door around nine or so, and when I took my hands off the keys and went over and opened it, Drew was standing there.

I raised my arms and slapped my hands against my sides fumingly. "For the love of Pete," I burst out. "You're not going to start in at this hour of the night, are you? I've told you over and over, as soon as I get something I'll give it to you. Can't you let up for one day at least?"

"Now wait a minute, wait a minute, don't get your back up," he tried to calm me. "D'you want to go to the movies?"

"What d'you mean, do I want to go to the movies?" I asked suspiciously.

He took a slip of paper out of his pocket. "I have a pass here for the R.K.O. Eighty-first Street. They send me one each week for letting them display their advertising down at the desk."

"It's for two," I said, glancing at it. "Are you coming with me?"

"I can't leave the hotel," he said. "My boss might take it into his head to call up or even drop around, and it would look bad if I weren't on the job. Take someone else with you. Take some girl."

"I can't take a girl," I said inflexibly. "It means an orangeade or a soda afterwards, that's the least you can do, and I can't even afford that much right now. It's too late to call anyone up at the last minute like this, anyway."

"Go by yourself then," he urged. "It'll do you good, relax you, take your mind off. You're leading an old man's life, C'nell, shut up in here day and night, night and day. You're only young once, mark my word, you'll regret it some day."

"No I won't," I contradicted him. "I've figured it all out. It's got to be now or later. I'd rather have it now and over with, and do my playing later."

But I took the pass from him and closed the door.

I buttoned up my shirt collar, put on a tie, slung my jacket across my arm, and went out—for the first time (except for just a hurried meal) in I don't know how many weeks.

I got as far as the corner, and then my feet seemed to lock themselves rigid on the pavement, wouldn't go on any further. I couldn't do it. I longed to see the show, as much as any school kid ever did who's only allowed to go once a week to a Saturday matinee—longed for a little fun and recreation, was almost famished for it—but I couldn't do it. My conscientiousness about first finishing the work I was doing was as rigid as an iron poker; I couldn't seem to bend it in the slightest.

I turned around and went back inside the hotel again and up to my room.

The door of the lady who lived on the other side of the hall from me was slightly ajar, and I could hear Drew's voice in there talking to her, as I came off the elevator.

He was taking his leave, and as he slowly came out backward, he didn't see me.

"—never lets up," she was complaining in a low, mournful voice. "Starts in at nine in the morning, and goes on all day long, sometimes until after twelve o'clock at night. I get the most splitting headaches from it. I've called down until I'm blue in the face, and it doesn't seem to do any good."

"Well, you won't have to listen to it tonight, at least," he promised her in a soothing voice. "I got rid of him for one night, anyway, by giving him a pass to a movie. Wish I'd have thought of it sooner."

"That's what you think!" I called out stridently.

He jumped almost a half foot off the floor, and whirled around, and his normally ruddy face got almost the color of a raspberry.

I shied the pass across the hall in his direction, keyed open my door, slammed it shut behind me, and went back to the typewriter keys again, with the renewed vigor of rancor now added to everything else.

Then suddenly one day there was a mystifying change in Mr. Drew's attitude. He beamed, his expression was cherubic, as we came unexpectedly face to face. He clapped my shoulder, he asked how I was, he winked at me to show a special geniality.

When I saw his extended hand, waiting for mine, I said with over emphasized weariness, "Now, please. *Don't* start that again. I've told you over and over: when I can, as soon as I can."

He looked hurt that I should misconstrue his friendliness. He creased his forehead ruefully. "C'nell, I haven't said a word. C'nell, have I said a word? Why do you jump on me like this?"

"No, but you're going to," I said skeptically.

"All I wanted to say was, now that you're caught up, try to stay that way. Don't let it run so far behind the next time."

"Next time?" I said dumbfounded. "What happened to this time?"

"Don't worry about it—" he started to say blandly.

"Don't worry about it?" I flared. "Now I *am* going to worry about it more than ever, because it's not like you to be so easygoing. There's something up. You're just trying to put me off my guard. I'll probably find my door plugged up when I come back."

"C'nell," he protested, horrified, raising a sanctimonious pudgy pink palm. Then he asked me, "Have you gotten a bill, all this week? Tell the truth now, have you?"

I suddenly realized I hadn't; they'd stopped. I was so used to ignoring them anyway, I hadn't noticed the difference.

"There you are," he went on. "You're in the clear. All paid up. Forget about it."

"Paid up?" I called after him loudly. "How can I be? Since when? Aren't you always dinning it into my ears that you don't know what you'll tell the owner when he comes around to collect his rents, that you don't know how you'll face him?"

But he was now, I could see, in as much of a hurry to get away from me as he had been before to approach me. I followed him a few steps, but I couldn't get another word out of him.

I couldn't make head nor tail out of this wholly improbable turn of events. I knew he was too good a hotel man to have mixed my account up with somebody else's, although for a moment that gratifying thought did cross my mind. I decided there was only one way to find out for sure, and that was to get a look at the hotel's bookkeeping ledger with my own eyes.

I knew that neither of the two daytime clerks would be likely to allow me to do that. They were too much under Drew's thumb. But the midnight-to-morning desk-man, Mr. Mack, was a far more unfettered spirit where Drew was concerned, since their hours did not coincide and they rarely saw one another. I might just possibly get him to do it if I went about it in the right way.

So late that night, shortly after he'd come on duty, I approached the desk, leaned negligently on my elbow and chatted with him for awhile. Then after I'd offered him a cigarette, I asked casually, "By the way, how does my bill stand? Do I still owe anything on it?"

He got out the bulky ledger, thumbed its pages over, scanned one, and then looked up at me. "You're paid up until the thirtieth of this month," he said.

"Let me see that," I exclaimed.

Caught off guard, just as I'd hoped, he let me turn it around my way without protest and trace my finger along the page. The entry was there as clear as day; the entire amount outstanding against me had been paid up, a matter of some five or six days earlier.

I didn't say anything more to him. I turned around and went back up to my room, almost in a daze.

I sat down and tried to think the thing out logically in my mind. The more I thought about it, the more convinced I became there was only one possible explanation, until finally I was sure I must be right.

Late the next afternoon, after I'd finished my daytime stint and before beginning my evening one, I went over to my mother's house to see her. I shouldn't actually call it her house; it had belonged to my grandfather, who had died six or seven years before, and his daughters had stayed on in it after that, both having lost their husbands.[12] My mother was the older, and (I suppose) the titular head of the small establishment.

The chow dog they kept in the house, Blong (or "Blong Mei," pidgin for "Belongs to Me," the name on his pedigree papers), always rushed clamoring against the door at anyone's ring, and then, when he'd hear my voice, would subside. But I always got the impression it was in a miffed sort of way, as though he felt cheated of having a chance to show his valor off before the two ladies who were in his charge.

"Are you going to have something with us?" was the first thing my mother asked after we'd kissed.

"No, I have to get right back," I told her. "You know I'm working on that thing."

"You're working too hard. You'll kill yourself. You've got to eat better."

And my aunt, tilting her head sideward to study me, concurred (as usual) with a plaintive "You don't look good. You looked better the last time you were here."

"Oh," I said impatiently, "I'll have all the rest of my life to eat in. The work comes first right now." Then I said to my mother, "I came over because I wanted to talk to you about something."

As soon as we were alone together in the other room, I told her: "I found out what you did."

A momentary flicker of guilt showed on her face, reminding me of the expression on a little girl's face when she has been found out doing something she knows she shouldn't. Then a look of quiet hurt took its place.

"That just shows you how reliable Mr. Drew is. He promised he wouldn't say anything."

"Drew didn't tell me," I said, and found myself for once in the odd position of defending my arch-enemy. "I got the night man to show me the ledger."

She didn't say anything to that.

"You don't carry that much around with you in your handbag at one time," I added. "You must have taken it out of your savings account."

"I went down to the bank the next day, after he'd spoken to me the last time I was over to see you, and I stopped off with it on my way home."

But I could only see it from my own point of view, no other. "I don't want to be helped," I insisted. "Don't you understand? I want to do this all on my own, prove to myself that I can do it, without any help from anyone. If you help me now, and I succeed afterward, then you've taken that much away from my success, made it that much less. I want it to be all mine. That's the only way I can really enjoy it if it comes." And I added with all that sublime, ridiculous cocksureness of one's young years, "I'm not going to sponge off anyone—not even my own mother."

I saw tears form in her eyes, but she kept them back.

"I don't understand you, the way you talk sometimes," she said quietly. "I only did it because I thought I would be helping you keep up your morale that way."

"But it's just the opposite; it's bad for my morale, instead of being good for it. Don't you have confidence in me?"

She came to me, put her arms around me, and pressed me fervently to her. "Every confidence!" she breathed. "You've got too much in you, not to be recognized some day. I only hope I live to see it, that's my one prayer."

"I know I'll make it," I chanted raptly. "I'm going to, and I will. I know this thing will work out right. It's got to." Then I said in a softer voice, "Promise me you won't do anything like that again."

"I won't, if you don't want me to," she said submissively. "But will you be all right?" she added with a touch of anxiety.

"Sure I will. I'm not afraid of Drew," I scoffed. "He's a great big coward, fat as he is."

"But he did turn the lights in your room off once, you told me."

"He won't try that again in a hurry," I assured her. "You should have seen me chase him all around the desk, in front of everybody standing there, until he sent the mechanic up and had him put the fuse back in again. It was like slapstick comedy; I'd go running in at one end and he'd come running out at the other, then he'd go running in again at the opposite end as I came out once more at the first one."

In retrospect, I can tell she didn't see the humor in it that I did. "I don't like you to be bad friends with him" was all she said, demurely.

Now that I'd gained my way in the major matter, I gave in on the minor one, not an uncommon trait in human nature. I stayed and had my meal with them, and they waited on me and handed me things at the table and made a lot of fuss over me, as they always did, and made me feel altogether like a king. Or at least like the lord of a manor visiting among his loyal and devoted tenantry.

But late that night when I was back in my own room, and through with my work, and going to bed, I thought again of what she, my mother, had done, and saw it in a different, truer perspective than I had at first, and the tears came to my own eyes for a moment, just as they had to hers.

I understood always, my whole life through, how much she loved me. And I think she understood, surely must have, how very much the same I felt about her.

On the night I finally came to the end of it, it was well on into the early morning hours. It seemed so quiet all at once, so smotheringly, stiflingly still, after all those days and nights and weeks of cricketlike chattering of the keys. Almost as though a thick eiderdown quilt had fallen down all over me, muffling everything. My ears couldn't seem to get used to it. They felt stunned, they almost seemed to be ringing with the emptiness. I'd stopped many times before this of course; stopped each night, and several times each day. But that was different, because then I knew I'd have to go on again each time. Now there was nothing more to come, the last keys had been struck, "The End" was lettered at the bottom of the final page, it was over. That's why, I suppose, I noticed the silence so much more than I had those other times. It was a psychological silence as much as an auditory one.

The hotel was asleep all around me. It was a quiet, drowsy sort of place anyway, most of the time. And even the street outside, which in that part of New York was, as a rule, never still, day or night, this night seemed to be so too, as if to blend itself in with my mood; just an occasional taxi-horn barking somewhere a block or so off. And the muffled surge of a lonely, passing subway train would now and then come up through the ventilating grids on the sidewalk and be plainly heard in the stillness of the streets above.

I turned the light out first, to cool my poor overworked eyes. It had been on so long, so steadily, that the heat of the glowing bulb extended all the way down the chain-pull to its very tip. When I touched that, it was hot enough to make me quickly take my fingers away. I sat there slumped before the desk in the dark for awhile, too tired even to get up and leave the chair. Then after awhile I made room by pushing things aside, and I laid my head down on the desktop, forehead first. I must have jarred the typewriter carriage slightly, and the little bell that always signalled the end of a line tinkled faintly, I remember. I thought it was a fitting coda to the whole thing. *Ping*, like that: and then unbroken silence.

I wanted desperately to go to sleep, and yet I was too keyed up, my nerves were too taut from the last long stint I'd put in, for me to be able to. Then suddenly hunger came. It struck me like a blow, almost. One moment there was no thought of food in my head, the next I was ravening.

I'd never felt hunger so strong, I'd never known it could be. It couldn't wait another moment, sleep was an impossibility until it was fed. It was agonizing. It was the actual pang I'd so often read of, but that I had never fully realized the meaning of before. It was like the teeth of an animal caught into you and refusing to let go their hold.

I dug into the linings of my pockets, quite unnecessarily. I'd already known I had no money. I had none. But this is not poetic license or retouching of a fact simply to point up, play up, a plight. This was literal: I had not one single, solitary penny of money on me, or in the room about me, or anywhere in the world, at that moment. The next day there would be some way of getting a little, there always was. But hunger couldn't wait until the next day. This wasn't one night's hunger, this was two months'. Even more, for that matter. I hadn't been eating well, even long before I'd first begun the book.

Now I thought of the poor strays who had come up to me on the street occasionally and asked me for enough money to get something to eat, and I was glad of the few times I'd been able to give it and sorry for the many times I'd had to refuse. But like most New Yorkers I'd been cynical, and thought they just wanted it for a drink. Tonight

I knew better; there must have been some of them at least who felt like I did now.

I got up, left the room, and closed the door behind me, about to do very much the same thing they had myself. Not on the streets, perhaps, but right here in the hotel itself—that was about the only difference. I went up to Drew's floor, two floors above my own, stood there for a moment mustering my courage, and then knocked on his door. I don't know yet—even as I stood there at the time I didn't—where I got the amazing gall, the effrontery, to single him out, of all people. Beneath all our squabbling and differences, there must have been some sense of empathy there.

It required quite some knocking, and of a steadily increasing caliber, before anything happened. Finally I heard his voice ask blurredly on the inside: "Who is it?"

For some indefinable reason, possibly a feeling of embarrassment, I couldn't bring myself to give my name, I just repeated my knock.

He opened the door and looked out at me, face puffed up rounded than ever with the swellings of sleep, eyes closed into slits, and in a dingy bathrobe.

"Help me out, will you?" I burst out impetuously. "I've got to have something to eat, I can't stand it—and I haven't got a cent. Lend me something, and I'll give it back to you. Even fifty cents. Anything."

He looked at me as though he thought he hadn't heard me right. "C'nell, are you crazy?" he gasped.

"Not crazy," I said, glowering at him. "Hungry. I'm crazed with hunger, yes."

He looked searchingly into my face, and I think he must have detected that I was practically drooling with the need for food. If my chin wasn't actually wet, the inside of my mouth kept filling with a saliva that I couldn't seem to dispose of.

Suddenly his wife called out from within their bedroom, "Charlie, who is that?"

"C'nell," he said, turning his head aside.

He tactfully didn't answer that. The two of us looked at each other with a sort of telepathic understanding. Husbandlike, he must have given her a faithful transcription of all our difficulties and all my derogations of him, and she could hardly have been a great admirer of mine.

Not getting any answer to her question, and not realizing that I could hear her where I was, or perhaps not caring, she called out, annoyed: "Tell him to go to grass!"

He made an inscrutable sign to me, and muffled his voice in precaution. "Too bad you woke her up. Wait here a minute. I'll see if I can get you something without letting her see me."

I stood there by the half-open door, and he went back toward the bedroom.

I heard her ask suddenly, as distinctly as ever, "Charlie, what are you doing over there?"

I quailed for a moment, as I know he too must have.

"I'm looking for my cigarettes, Cass," I heard him say to her.

Then he came back to the door again and, with his head turned watchfully in her direction, put a dollar bill into my hand.

I didn't know what to say to him. "I'm sorry" was all I could think of. "I'm sorry about all the times I've rowed with you and insulted you. It won't happen any more, after this."

"Forget about it, boy," he said, and he gave me one of the usual claps on the shoulder, but at the same time I saw him shaking his head to himself. "I didn't realize. You really are hard up, aren't you?"

Her final voicing aloud put an end to our bathos-redolent reconciliation scene. "Charlie, come back to bed!" she called out in no uncertain terms.

He quickly closed the door, and I as quickly went away from it.

I went up the street one block and across, where there was a cafeteria that stayed open all night. I ordered scrambled eggs and coffee and sat down to them, moaning under my breath with a peculiar mixture of pain and pleasure. The tabletops were white glazed, and stained with unwiped food marks. The sugar was caked in the sugar sifters. The coffee had been reboiled a hundred times. Still, I'd eaten a thousand times before then, and I've eaten a thousand times since then, but no food I've ever had tasted as good as the coffee in that inch-thick mug and the eggs on that greasy cracked plate that I ate in that cheap cafeteria at three or four o'clock that morning. It tasted the way food should taste. I almost wanted to cry with gratitude, it tasted so good.

Then I went back to my room and fell into the bottomless, prostrated sleep of release from months of accumulated fatigue and overwork.

I took the book downtown the next day and turned it over to Irwin, and the rest was only to wait.

I found the waiting harder than the working almost. For my life hadn't changed; the same scrimping, scraping, cutting down on meals to save a penny went on as before. Never any money, at least not enough all at a time to do anything with. And now that the solar plexus of the book had been taken out of my life, there was a great big hole left in the middle of it. I didn't know what to do with myself. I couldn't start working on something else because there wasn't the remotest possibility of selling anything else right then, and even if there had been, I still couldn't have; I was too drained by the effort I had just put in, I needed a breathing spell first.

Every night I would go out walking, killing time, merged in the drifting crowd I used to glimpse so longingly from my window. Yes, people still strolled the avenues in the Depression evenings, even if they couldn't do anything else. The lights were as gay as ever, the voices as animated, the smiles as ready, even if the hearts weren't quite as light anymore. The lights would be rippling on the picture-theatre marquees like sprays of colored water, glinting in furriers' show-windows, which were coated with amber-tinted cellophane (a new decorative device then). The lights would be sizzling on casefuls of zircons and rhinestones like glassed-in fireworks displays. The lights would be shining from below upward, like submerged crocuses, at the feet of posturing mannequins garbed in the by-now universal silhouette of the new day: skirts to the shin and shoulders squared off and padded like those of a football player's uniform. And hair brushed flat from side to side across the top like that of a little girl of seven.

Even when they couldn't buy half the things they looked at, it was nice just to look, and the same went for me.

Then when they were tired of walking, they could always go back home and listen to the Kate Smith program, or the Eddie Cantor show, or Burns and Allen, and that was free of charge too.[13] I could do that too; the only difference was I couldn't sit down or take my coat off. I'd sold my little Emerson portable radio long before, but I used to get all the programs by standing in the entrances of hospitable music stores that had their loudspeakers turned on over the doorway. The jokes were just as funny there.

Life was as good as ever, as good as it's always been, to me and to those strolling with me. The only difference was you needed money more than you once had, for there was now far less of it around. But there wasn't one of us in that promenading-to-nowhere-and-back crowd who would have changed it, changed life, for anything else.

Each night when I went to bed, I said to myself, "Maybe tomorrow he'll call." Then the day came, and he didn't, and the night came, and again; "Maybe tomorrow. Maybe tomorrow."

A dozen times, a half a hundred times, I started to call him instead, and I kept from doing so. A dozen times I already had my nickel in the pay slot, and I pressed down the arm and brought it back to me again. Once I even got through to his office, and then I wouldn't name myself to the switchboard operator, hung up before she could put me through.

For I knew it wouldn't help any, wouldn't hasten it any, might even detract from it if I become too importunate or impatient. One call would bring on a second, then a third, and each time less and less gained. He would call me when he was ready, when the decision had been reached, and he wouldn't call me before. My calling him wouldn't make the decision; only his calling me would.

So until then it had to be "Maybe tomorrow he'll call me. Maybe tomorrow he'll call."

And then suddenly one morning he did. Very early, very unexpectedly, about 9:30 in the morning. It must have been almost as soon as he reached his desk. I'd jumped straight to the phone from my bed, and it was only as the film strips of sleep peeled slowly off my mind one by one that I realized whose the voice was. I stood there, holding up my pajama pants with one hand, the phone in the other.

"You sound half awake," I heard him say. "Can you come down here later in the day?" he said. "I'd like to talk to you. I'd ask you to lunch, only I'm doing without lunches these days."

I was fully awake by now and almost bursting with excitement. "Forget lunch!" I told him. "What about the book? Is it in? Is it in?"

"Wait'll you get your eyes open, then come down," he hedged. "I don't like talking on the phone anyway. It's much more satisfactory when you get together personally." And he hung up.

I tried to click him back on again, but he was off for good and I couldn't get him back.

I let go my pajama waistband and it fell down to the floor and I had to bend over and hoist it up again.

It can't be a rejection, I kept thinking as I dressed, and then later as I rode the excruciatingly slow subway, or he would have told me then and there. I knew editors well enough by now; in that case he would rather *not* have had me come down and see him.

When I stepped into his office, the first thing I noticed was that it wasn't in evidence, he didn't have it there on his desk ready to give back to me, and my hopes rose even higher still.

He started in by mentioning its good points, bouncing a pencil on its end as he remarked each one.

"It's gay, it's jaunty.

"There's only one trouble. It's no longer valid.

"That Paris is gone."

"That Paris'll never be gone," I retorted resentfully, much as you refute a slander against the personality of your first sweetheart—such as that she's aging, no longer what she used to be.

"Yes it is," he insisted. "It's as dead as the New York that used to send half its own population over there to visit every summer. That's beside the point anyway. We're not selling the book in Paris, we're selling it right here in New York. People aren't going to read it there, they're going to read it here. And the New York that used to want to read about that Paris doesn't exist anymore."

He was right; I could see with my own eyes that it didn't.

"It's out," I murmured, releasing a long, mournful sigh.

He didn't answer.

"Well, where is it, then?" I finally wanted to know. "I may as well take it home with me."

He opened his desk drawer and fumbled around a little, but more as though making time than actually looking for something which he really didn't know where to locate. Then instead of the thick 300-odd-page typescript, he brought out a single sheet of paper with a few lines typed on it.

"I know you want to make money on it," he remarked.

I didn't answer that; it was too obvious.

He handed me the slip of paper to read.

It very briefly stated, in no more than two or three typed lines: In the event of a sale of my book, "I Love You, Paris" to X-Studios on the recommendation of Mr. Y, Associate Producer at that studio, I agreed to divide the profits of the sale fifty-fifty with Mr. Irwin—.

"You keep all the other rights just as much as ever," he hastened to assure me. "In fact, they might even reconsider here and do it as a book, if a successful motion picture comes out of it. That's been done before. A successful motion picture helps to sell a book, you know."

Then he went on to tell me that he knew this Mr. Y, and was sure that if he liked it a sale could be made on the strength of his recommendation to the studio heads. It was not like sending it to an agent. This was a direct contact with the studio itself.

I didn't need much more urging than that. I signed it and he put it back where he'd taken it from.

Then and only then he told me, "It's already out there. We ought to hear any day now. I know you need the money, don't want to be held up too long waiting."

We shook hands, and my hopes went way up again, even higher than they'd been before.

On that note I left him and went home.

I knew I hadn't been too astute, but I felt I hadn't had much choice in the matter, and anyone else in my position would have done pretty much as I had. Certainly, I was giving away half my potential profits. But I was giving away half of nothing, for without him and his associate-producer friend Mr. Y, there would be no chance of a sale at all, I knew. Half a cake, to be La Rochefoucauldian about it, was better than none.[14]

At that, he could have been much more demanding, or let's say much more flagrant, about it. By that I mean he could have insisted on a half share of any picture sale at all that was made, and not just a sale to the one studio that was specified. Or worse still, he could have bought the book outright from me, all rights to it, for a thousand dollars or even five hundred dollars of his own (which I'm not sure I would have been able to refuse) and thus stand to collect the entire amount when the sale came. But I suppose, to be completely objective about it, he didn't have the thousand or five hundred in his own pocket, and couldn't very well ask the publishers for it since they'd already turned the book down.

I think all it amounted to was that he saw a chance to make some money on his own account out of something that had fortuitously come his way, and took it. And who is to blame him? I could see his logic, and I didn't resent it in the least.

I'm only trying to be fair. It doesn't matter now anymore, but it mattered terribly then.

I went home again to wait. This second wait was even worse than the first, for it was added to the first, was a continuation of it, and therefore seemed to have gone on twice as long as it actually had. But I outlasted it, I outlived it. Everything comes to an end, and at last it did too.

When he called me this time, he did it indirectly. He had his assistant—he seemed to have attained the status of having his own secretary by now, or perhaps it was just the general operator for the office—put the call through for him, and he didn't get on himself. She asked if I could come down that afternoon, said he'd like to see me. I said I would, of course, but when I asked if I could talk to him himself, she told me that he was either tied up in a meeting or had stepped out of the office for a short while, I forget now which it was. Which could have been perfectly true, after all.

I let it go at that; what difference did an extra hour or two make, after all those leaden-footed days and weeks I'd put in waiting?

On my way to his office from the subway stop, I took a shortcut through a side-street. As I was moving briskly along through it, the figure of a middle-aged woman descending a short flight of stone steps just ahead of me caught my eye. She was shrouded completely in black, apparently in widow's weeds, but the brief glimpse I had of her face as she turned away and went up the street before me had showed a serenity, a passivity, that struck me. It was a sad cast of expression with its downlidded eyes, but it was completely at peace, that much couldn't be doubted.

I glanced at the steps, and then up above them. The cool, dingy and yet dignified facade of a Church met my eyes. I had never yet been inside one. Neither for any joyous occasion nor any sad one. Neither for a wedding nor a funeral, a baptism nor a confirmation nor a mass.[15]

I stopped, and turned halfway, and stood there looking at it. Then I moved slowly back again the few steps past it that I'd gone, and stood and looked some more.

People went into them for help; why shouldn't I? That woman I'd seen just now had, and you could tell by her face that she'd found it, been given what she asked.

But, something inside me argued, that woman's concerns are with death, her black garb shows that. Yours are with life and life only; it isn't the same thing.

I loitered around out there thinking the thing out, a sort of sidewalk loafer in front of a church, my hands deep in my pockets in uncertainty, the inevitable cigarette clenched in my mouth.

My sense of fair play, my sense of good manners, told me: You shouldn't go in just when you have something to ask for. You should have been going in steadily all along before now. Then you would be entitled to go in now and ask for your favor. This way you're not. You're only trying to use God. It's your problem, you should keep it to yourself.

Everyone uses God. Why shouldn't I? Every prayer that was ever sent up is asking God a favor. Why shouldn't my prayer go up too, along with all the other millions? I'm entitled to my happiness as much as anyone else.

Then another thought came to further cloud the issue: You wouldn't let your mother help you. You claimed it would take something away from you. Then why are you willing to let God help you? Won't that also take something away from you?

It's not the same thing, I answered in thought. My mother is weaker than I am, God is stronger. My mother looks up to me, admires me. God certainly doesn't. When you let the weaker help you, you detract from yourself. When you let the stronger help you, you don't. If you see a small child fall flat and lie there on the ground bawling, and you go over and help it back to its feet, do you detract from that child?

I threw my cigarette over my shoulder, jerked my hands out of my pockets, and ran tautly up the steps, neck slightly bent, as though they were a springboard into a pool of icy-cold water.

I had a fleeting impression of a marble-floored vestibule with a stone basin of water (was that what they called holy water? I wondered) set between two massive inner doors, and then I was standing stock still in the dim interior, as suddenly as I'd surged forward from outside just now.

The hush was the first thing I noticed about it. There was some sort of an inner quiet here that other buildings didn't have, for surely its walls were no thicker than many of theirs and yet they lacked it. The absence of windows? I asked myself. Far ahead, it seemed, there were little taper-lights. They seemed to be up on the wall, although I knew they actually weren't. They reminded me of shimmering teardrops and little ruddy drops of blood that had trickled down a certain distance, and then stopped and stayed there, pulsing, each one where it was.

Finally I moved again. I didn't go too far forward, I was too timid to. I think subconsciously I was fearful somebody would come out from the side, down there by the altar, and ask me what I was doing in there, what right I had to be in there.

I chose about the fourth or fifth row from the back, entered it, and sat down three or four seats from the outside. I clasped my hands and rested them on the back of the seat in front of me, and just sat for awhile, my head respectfully lowered a trifle, but taking everything in from under my eyelids. It had a tragic grandeur to it, and yet an infinite loneliness too. I wondered if the next world was going to be this lonely. People took your loneliness away; God made you feel vastly lonely.[16] I wondered why that was; it should be the other way around, I thought, shouldn't it?

My unaccustomed mundane eye, no conscious irreverence intended, kept traveling in the direction of the altar and expecting to come up against a big, blank picture-screen that was not to be found there. The cavernous grandiloquence was like that of a large motion-picture palace before the audience has filed in and the cameras have started turning in the projection room. I kept trying to put the thought out of my head, but it kept coming back again each time. It was the only comparison my past experience could conjure up.

I brought one knee down to the floor, but since that was an awkward position—there wasn't space enough there to comfortably allow the length of a bent leg—I finally brought the other one down beside it, and crouched there like that, my forehead pillowed against my clasped hands.

I had common sense enough to realize that formula didn't matter, it wasn't what counted. I knew no stylized prayers or forms of addressing God, because I'd never used any. And even words, that is, unspoken words within my mind, were difficult to marshal. So I contented myself with offering my prayer in thought form only, letting the smooth-flowing current of my thoughts carry it along far more evenly and naturally than any word-forms could have.

It was about like this:

"Dear God: Nature or You—if you are separate, and I don't think you are, or both—have put an unusually strong love of life in me. Everybody has it, I know, but I have it to an inordinate degree. And by love of life, I don't mean just the act of breathing and the wish not to stop breathing. I mean having fun, having a good time.

"My youthfulness is about to end, and I myself robbed it of many of the years it was entitled to.

"That's why I ask you: let me have this money now, while I can still enjoy it as it should be enjoyed, to the hilt. Five years from now will be too late. Or even four. Even three.

"I don't want it for security. I don't want it to hoard, or put away in a musty bank, or count over or scheme with. I want it to live with.

"Let me have it now.

"Now.

"Now, or not at all."

I noticed a strange thing immediately afterward. I felt strangely emptied out, weak, as when you've just expended all the energy you're capable of. I knew by that, whatever my prayer's merits, whatever its importunity, whatever its impertinence, it had been at least sincere, not feigned, not superficial, not play-acting.

I stayed there as I was for some time afterwards, too limp to move, and I noticed that there were beads of perspiration on my forehead, and I felt moist under the arms.

After awhile I passed my sleeve across my forehead and dried it off, and got stiffly and clumsily back to a sitting position. I say again, I meant that prayer with all my heart and all my soul.

Finally, as the pressures of the outside world began to circle closer around me again, and particularly as the imminence and importance of my appointment with Irwin came back to mind, I got to my feet and moved haltingly backwards out of the space between the seats. Why backwards, I haven't any idea. Possibly I thought it was the proper etiquette.

I went up the aisle and outside into the streets, and the sudden onset of their life-noises was almost like being buffeted by a howling storm, the first few minutes, after the unearthly silence inside there.

The effect (not of the noise but of the emotion spent) hadn't altogether worn off yet even by the time I reached Irwin's office. I could tell that by the meek, almost limp way I went in, when the girl ushered me, and shook hands and submissively sat down opposite him, instead of rushing in with all sorts of questions popping from my lips as I ordinarily would have.

He came directly to the point, now that he had me in front of him. (And I have never been able to understand that telephonic indirectness, evasiveness, of his, then or since.)

"Cornell," he said, "I wish I had something good to tell you. It's back. It came in this morning."

"Oh," I said almost inaudibly. "It's turned down."

"Turned down," he repeated. And then he went on to discuss their viewpoint briefly. The post-mortem was of no value even then, and still less now, so there is no point in repeating it.

Finally he said, "I want to show you that I'm trying to be fair about this," and he took out the single sheet of paper granting him half share of the rights which I had signed the previous time, had me glance at it, then tore it into four pieces and dropped them into his wastebasket.

I think this only made me feel worse, instead of reassuring me as he had probably intended it to, for it only pointed up to my mind how hopeless from a sales angle he must consider the thing to be, to do that.

True, the grant had been valid only in this one instance, but I was in no mood to derive any comfort from that. If he had thought there was any further chance, he wouldn't have relinquished it so easily.

"It was a one-shot," he pointed out. "And when a one-shot goes wrong, it goes wrong, and that's all there is."

"Yeah," I assented bitterly.

The thing was beginning to sink slowly in, and I could feel myself hardening up. I realized the best thing I could do was get out of there, before I started taking it out on him. He actually hadn't done anything wrong, I kept reminding myself, only what I had intended doing myself from the beginning; if anything, he'd expedited it.

The last thing I recall saying to him was: "I even went into a church and prayed I'd have luck with it."

I've never forgotten what he answered to that. "You must have picked the wrong church," he smiled cynically.

So I left there, as the defeated always leave the place of their defeat: heavy-hearted, leaden-footed, the world all black and stormy around me, not a ray of light in it anywhere.

All that hard work for nothing. All those wearisome drudging weeks. A whole big chunk taken out of my life and thrown away, wasted. But far worse than the disappointment itself was the timing of it. My instinct told me very surely that this marked the ending of something or other in me. Call it being young, call it being completely carefree. Call it being wholeheartedly foolish, even; that has its place in life too. And I knew that that was the real reason why I'd prayed. Not just for the money itself, for its own sake. (That would have been too presuming even for my non-theological turn of mind.) But to be given the money now, when every penny would have brought a dollar's worth of zest and enjoyment, and not later, when every dollar would bring only a penny's worth, maybe not even that much.

I noticed an ashcan standing by the curb as I came out of the building and made my downcast way along the street. I opened the clasp-envelope he had so bountifully given me and took my manuscript out of it.

I took the title page, which had my name on it, off it first, and crumpled that into a ball and jammed it down into my pocket. Then I dropped the rest of it, just as it was, bodily into the ashcan.

Then I scooped some of the powdery white ash over it and covered it up. Buried it, as it were.

Then I went on without it, but I felt heavier, not lighter, than when I'd been carrying it.

I came across a bar, and I went in. What more natural place to go, at such a time and in such a frame of mind? But I couldn't even drown my sorrows adequately. I had just enough for one beer on me, plus the nickel required for the long subway trip up to the hotel.

There was no one else in the place at that hour of the afternoon, and the bartender must have unnoticeably taken in my dismal expression as I lingered there, head bowed numbly over the lone beer until it was gone. I suppose he guessed my dejection had to do with money in one way or another. Everyone's did in those days.

When he saw me start to sidle off the stool about to go, he called over from where he was standing: "Have another."

"I can't," I said. "That's all I have enough for."

"Have one on me, then," he invited, and I glimpsed a rueful cast of compassion on his face for just a moment as he brought it over and set it down before me. That told me it wasn't just business goodwill that prompted him, it was human sympathy. Sympathy for a kid, of an older man who's gone through the same thing himself and knows what it's like. Nothing further was said by either one of us. When I finished it, I nodded to him and went out. But the trifling little act of human fellowship had made me feel better.

Not much, just an infinitesimal bit better. Like when your leg is broken, and you're lying there, and somebody pats his handkerchief to your moist forehead. It doesn't make the pain any less, but at least you're not alone in the pain.

A moment after, I turned around and went back to the place again.

I flung the door forcefully inward without, however, releasing my hold on it, not wanting it to strike back and break his glass.

"Y'know something, mister," I called in to him.

He turned, startled slack-jawed.

"No, wh-what?" he quavered, half frightened, I could tell, by my unexpected vehemence.

"You're better, even, than God. Because God didn't give me a ten-cent glass of beer free. But you did!"

And I reclosed the door and went on my bitter, beaten, homeward way, freed forever of any further religious beliefs.

There is a brief postscript to this story. Somewhat under a year later, which would bring it up to about 1934, a new picture opened in one of the first-run picture houses downtown. It had the word "Paris" somewhere in its title, that much I can recall. But that was nothing; the important thing about it was the reviews, which I read the next day just as I always did after any new opening. They were not overly enthusiastic about it, but they all alike mentioned that at least one thing in its favor, if not the only one, was that it brought a fresh and hitherto untouched period to the screen: the 1912 epoch.

I immediately went down there to see it. There were variations in it here and there, of course; there always are in any film derivation, even when its source has been bought and paid for. But its two leading characters were still a pair of ballroom dancers, and they still danced their highlight number to the rhythm of Ravel's "Bolero" just as I had specified in my script.[17] As for the dialogue, much of that had been transposed almost verbatim. Not just a few random remarks, but whole stretches, especially in the key scenes. I couldn't fail to recognize it. I had worked too hard to try to make it witty, scintillating, brittle. It came out now sounding flat and dull to my discouraged ears, but it was still my dialogue, superimposed upon a very close approximation of my plot, set in the Paris of, not the year 1911, not the year 1913, but 1912. In fact, throughout it bore such an unabashed verisimilitude to my piece that it almost looked as though somebody had been paid for it. But it certainly hadn't been I.

I came out of there with a sullen scowl on my face, but actually it no longer hurt. That had been last year's grief and heartache. I was already starting on the way up again myself by now. I had no time for last year's grief, I was too taken up in this year's hopes and plans. And there was this note of consolation to be derived from it too: whoever had stolen it, had stolen it as much from Irwin as from me. It had, in actuality, been stolen twice over. The biter had been bitten in turn.

It no longer hurt.

IV
President Eisenhower's Speech

In "President Eisenhower's Speech," the garish unreality of hotel life heightens a claustrophobic power struggle between Woolrich and his ailing mother. Despite the almost trivial plot, this chapter provides a vivid portrait of Woolrich's psychological relationship with his mother, alternating between protection and entrapment, secrecy and revelation, love and death.

One frantic day in 1957, a matter of months before his mother's death, Woolrich sought to protect her from the hotel fire raging beneath a distracting presidential radio address. The story shows these two residents of a small hotel suite finding small ways to assert their independence, while vainly hoping to deny a binding dependency they feel for each other.

During most of Woolrich's adult life, after the failure of his unconsummated 1930 marriage to Gloria Blackton, until his mother's death in October 1957, they shared two or three small rooms in one of a series of Manhattan hotels. Woolrich's will specified that he be buried in the double crypt with his mother's remains after his own death in 1968.

One can only assume that this account typifies the nature of their emotional life together during all those years.

At nine o'clock that Wednesday evening, which was the twentieth of February, 1957, the President was to make a nationwide speech over the radio.[1] This had been announced some days before, as such things always are. When she heard of it my mother expressed an interest in listening in, and she mentioned it again as we sat at the table, a short while before the time scheduled for it to begin, I suppose in order to make sure it didn't escape my mind. But I had no intention of neglecting to put it on. It would have been difficult to avoid it, in any case, if one were to use the radio at all, for it was being carried by all four of the major networks and most of the smaller ones as well. However, she had too little diversion during the course of the tedious, protracted convalescence she was undergoing at the time for me to wish to deny her the privilege of listening. And I wanted to hear it myself, though perhaps with less of an intrinsic faith in whatever it was he had to say. For she belonged to the generation of wholehearted national loyalties, pre-1914, and I belonged to the generation of wearied international cynicism, post-Munich.[2]

I had better explain that though she was not incapacitated in any degree—had full use of her limbs at all times and moved about the rooms at will—she had had a massive and almost fatal heart-attack less than a year before and had not been out of the apartment since. But the doctor, who came weekly, was finding steady improvement, and had promised that when the milder weather came around again she could go outdoors once more for a short while every day. Needless to say it was extremely inadvisable for her to move about too hurriedly, no matter what the occasion, or under the spur of any undue stress or fear or excitement. I had made it my job to keep such things at as great a distance as possible from her.

This was the situation that existed as we put our emptied coffee cups back upon the table that night. I helped her to a more comfortable chair (the radio was in the same room in which we took our meals), and turned the dial to one of the stations at random.

There were a few moments of dead air, as it is called in radio terminology, evidently the pause after whatever it was that had just ended. Then the national anthem began to play. Since we were alone in our own home, with only the eyes of God, let us say, upon us, I did not rise to my feet, no disrespect intended however; and she on her part was exempted from doing so by her infirm condition.

The music stopped.

"Ladies and gentlemen, the President of the United States," the announcer intoned.

An impressive pause followed.

Then the President's voice sounded.

"My Fellow Citizens," he began, "May I first explain to you that for some days I have been experiencing a very stubborn cough, so if because of this I should have to interrupt myself this evening, I crave your indulgence in advance. I come to you again to talk about the situation in...."

Almost from his opening words I detected some flaw in the clarity of the reception we were getting. His own voice was perfectly audible, in actual fact more than just audible: ringingly, resoundingly clear, even reverberant, you might say. But instead of the knell-like silence that should have backed his voice, there was a curious blurry confusion somewhere in his immediate vicinity that the microphones were picking up and sending out along with his own august utterances. It was intermittent, would rise and fall, at times seem to disappear, then come back again more strongly than ever. One part of it was like a drone or hum, as when many far-off voices are all sounding together. Another part held in it the sound of bells clanging. They too were intermittent like the voices, and they too were muted like the voices. They were not like church bells, they were more like wild, rollicking New Year's Eve bells. And yet why bells at all, I wondered? They didn't seem an appropriate accompaniment for a Presidential speech.

"Do you notice that?" I said to my mother finally. "I wonder what it is?" I went over and tried adjusting the dial slightly, but the noise persisted.

"Where is he speaking from?" she asked me, without saying whether she did notice it or not. But she was at all times of a more even, patient temperament than I.

"I don't know," I said. "It sounds as though he's at some big, noisy banquet. Such sounds should be filtered out by the people at the controls."

I kept fiddling with the knob, as you do at such times, but that only made him less sharp and the background noises more so. I moved over to another station, but since there was only one point of origin for the speech, no matter what the station was, its imperfections of transmission were bound to be carried by all of them alike.

She seemed content with it as it was, and not nearly as impatient about it as I. I finally desisted, hoping it would clear up by itself later on, as such "bugs" often do in radio. I sat back resignedly, crossed my legs, lighted a cigarette, and settled down to listen as patiently as I could, interference or no interference. For just a moment, a moment only. Then something made me get up again and walk out of the room, without saying anything to her. I can't say exactly what it was. It wasn't tangible or defined enough to be called a suspicion or even a premonition. Just a stray thought, entering my mind from nowhere, and acted upon by motor reflex.

I went into the front room, which was a corner room with a fine double exposure, and threw open one of the windows on the side-street side. Although the hotel fronted on Broadway, its entrance was around on this side-street. The windows in the other room were floor-length, opening like doors, and the night was cold as a knife. I didn't want the inflowing air to play about my mother's feet.

Before I even had a chance to bend my head out through the opening and look down (for we were on a fairly high floor, the street was extremely narrow, and the tall buildings lining both sides turned it into little better than a chasm, I found out where the aberrations on the radio were coming from. They were coming from outside on the street, all around the hotel.

The night air wasn't as cold-tipped as my heart when I looked down and saw what was down there. The entire length of the side-street was choked from one end to the other with fire-fighting apparatus, some of it already in position, some just in the act of reaching the scene, and all alike clamoring with the throb of heavy engines and the clang of equally heavy bells as they settled one by one into silence, until all alike were silent, with a silence that was more excruciating than any noise, a portentous, biding silence. And meanwhile satanic red headlight beams whisked back and forth across the faces of the onlooking buildings like bloodied rapiers and sometimes intercrossed in swinging counter to one another, as though engaged in some pyromaniac duel.

Those were the bells, the bells of celebration that the radio cabinet had seemed to give out as its own.

A crowd was rapidly forming even in that biting temperature, but it was being held back within bounds by the police, at first with handlinked outstretched arms, then later with lengths of rope looped over movable traffic stanchions, to restrict it to the opposite sidewalk, across the street from the hotel, and to the various doorways and raised entry steps and whatever niches there were in the building fronts over on that side. In these the crowd clustered, looking (seen from above) like round fat black bees, sucking excitement like drops of honey from that which was misery and misfortune to others. Windows squares were starting to light up here and there, over on that side, too, and people to look out through them and to beckon to others who had still remained back within the rooms to come forward and join them in looking. I could see some of them doing it.

And all these, of course, were the voices of the banqueters in the background that had seemed to be coming from the radio transmitter. (And maybe in a sense they were banqueters after all.)

Worse by far than any of the rest of it, however, was the sight of the crew of one of the just-arrived fire trucks jumping down from it like a handful of pebbles scattered all over the street, running full tilt for the hotel entrance, and disappearing under the overhang of its canopy, some carrying axes at the ready, others the writhing coils of a thick, anaconda-like hose, that acted like something alive as it wriggled and tossed about under their multiple holds. It was the headlong pace at which they raced inside that to me was the appalling thing about it, for, although I realized that firemen could not at any time be expected to stroll or amble casually toward a fire, these men were speeding with a terrible, wordless intensity, as though every second were priceless. I could see that much even from up where I was; the very downslant of their figures and rigid forward bend of their heads told it. I couldn't escape the foreboding thought, in view of this, that, although every fire in an occupied building is an emergency, true enough, this must be an emergency of the very worst sort, to make them leap forward like that.

And over and above everything else there was the hollow, doom-like sound of the two-way radio on one of the vehicles, echoing dismally upward into the reaches of the night, reporting over and over at staccato intervals the location, the exact address, before which they stood now. This somehow added an extra touch of horror all its own. For we *lived* there. That was where we *lived*. Fires took place in other people's houses, not where you lived yourself.[3]

I absorbed all this with one long, sustained stare, not piecemeal as I've had to tell it, but as on a sweeping cyclorama flowing unbroken before my eyes. And though it must have lasted several good minutes at least, to me it seemed as swift and instantaneous as the quick flash of fear that it felt like.

My first thought was of my mother, inside in the other room, unaware and unprotected. No, that isn't accurate; to be a first, there must be a second, an afterthought. There was just the one thought, of her.

Even mere knowledge of the situation we suddenly found ourselves in, by itself, could be dangerous to her, might bring on the second—and possibly final—attack I had been dreading so all these months. Just the knowledge—much less the high-pitch tension sure to be connected with any abrupt and unstabilizing removal to a safer place (even had it been physically feasible for me to carry her out unaided, which it was not), or the commotion or perhaps even electrically contagious panic likely to be met with on the way, the subfreezing temperature outside the building, or finally—and this was most important of all—any inhalation of smoke to the slightest degree. There were all these things.

Then knowledge must be kept from her for as long as it could be. There was no other way, that was the only way. And keeping it from her was up to me, was my task, my assignment.

In this I had one great advantage. A matter of just a few weeks before this, she had developed a minor impairment of hearing. It was not a basic defect, the doctor had assured me on examining her, but simply a question of the wax which is normally found deep within the eardrum having failed to dislodge itself properly. He told me he could have cleared it up then and there by use of a small instrument, but since it was bound to correct itself within another week or so at the most, he preferred to let nature do the work for him, she being the best and gentlest doctor of them all. At close range my mother's hearing remained unaffected. She could hear what I said and listen to the radio (obviously) with no difficulty whatever. But at a greater distance, such as a room away, for instance, some of the edge had been taken off her keenness of hearing, and many sounds now escaped her, particularly if they were in a minor key. It was in this very way, as a matter of fact, that I had first become aware of the condition, noticing one day after I had keyed open and then released the outside door after me that she did not turn her head to see who it was, from where she sat beside a window in the front room.

It was on this that I pinned my hopes of successfully carrying out what I had in mind. If such a detriment had to be at all, then this was the whole excuse for its being. It was made to order for just such an emergency as tonight's. That is, to keep the off-center sounds of what was going on—or at least the meaning of them—from her for so long as I could.

I closed the window very quietly and carefully, so that if she had not heard me open it (as I trusted she hadn't), she would not know I had been near it at all. The crackling frosty-sharp noise from the street was cut off as at the throw of a switch, or at least muffled to a soft, subtle blur. I decided, as I moved away from the window, that if she had heard the commotion and asked me what it was, I would say that it was nothing much, nothing to do with us; either that it was a few doors up the street from us, or that it had been a false alarm turned in at our own building and they were already leaving the scene. If she had not heard, I would of course say nothing. Just wait and see, borrowing minute from minute, until either it grew so bad I couldn't put off telling her any longer or it was over and there was nothing any longer to tell.

Her face, I was sure, would tell me whether she had heard it or not.

I moved back into the room very slowly and casually, trying to give the appearance of aimlessly strolling about the apartment without any purpose in mind. The President's voice rolled gravely and decorously on. She was sitting in a relaxed posture. She was absorbed in listening. I could see that, by the way her eyes scarcely moved toward me as I re-entered. My cigarette was smoking away there in the tray where I had left it. The room was like a little cubicle of calm after the bedlam outside the window.

I knew she could not have heard.

I let out a deep breath of heartfelt relief, slouched down into the chair with exaggerated languor, picked up the cigarette, drew on it once, put it down again.

"And we shall in this great effort seek the association of other like-minded nations—" he was saying.[4]

I got slowly to my feet again, as if I were incurably restless, drifted over to the doorway, through it, and out of the room. Once the doorway was obscuringly between us, I sped with a bound across the foyer, jerked back the front door, looked out.

It wasn't reassuring. There was already a very thin haze noticeable in the hotel corridor. Worse than that however were the figures coming and going, seen through it like flitting shadows. Returning to their rooms for something, coming out of their rooms again, all very quickly, like puppets jerked on strings and not at all the way people ordinarily move. I saw a man standing waiting down by the elevator doors, which were midway along the hall from us, for the car to come by for him, with his child held in his arms wrapped in a blanket, another child a little larger standing beside his leg holding onto it with both small arms.

I knew him by sight, and to say good evening to. He was a nice man; a decent, honest man. A very poor man, obviously, but he carried his poverty with a manly sort of dignity that almost made it seem a distinction and not a lack. There was a third child—and a wife, of course. They weren't with him right then, they must have already been downstairs by this time. He had one of the smallest rooms on the floor, for the five of them, with just a washstand in it. And the array of beds in it, when I glimpsed the inside once or twice through the open door in passing, made it seem even smaller than it was, with the floor area all swallowed up. But his wife was a scrupulously clean woman, and on a line which she had strung up along one entire side of the room there would be hanging an assembly of freshly washed children's clothes so long it almost tired the eye to follow it.

Yet somehow you never thought of pitying these people; their own attitude of sturdy integrity, of lack of self-pity, rejected it and made it seem uncalled for.

I closed my own door behind me first as a precaution, in order to avoid being overheard inside, and then I called down toward him— I had to call out, not just speak, for the hall was a long one—"How bad is it?"

"I don't know," he called back. "But I thought I better get the kids out, anyway."

I didn't blame him in the least for that. Secretly, I even envied him. Just pick up the thing you cherished the most and carry it safely out of the building with you in your arms. I couldn't do that, that was denied me.

The brighter light from the elevator spilled across him and his two children like a flare—for the hall-lights were small and dim at all times, even when it was smokeless out there—showing by indirection when the slide door had opened before his face. And packed as the rickety little box of an elevator must have been (I could hear the surf-like surging sound that a great many voices all going at once make), he managed to wedge first the children and then himself onto it. Then the slide door, which operated automatically, wouldn't reclose, because too many were on, and their arms or their elbows or their shoulders or their feet were in the way of its trajectory.

But no one would be the first one to step off, to clear the way so that it could go down with all the others. And what a senseless sort of cowardice that was, too, I couldn't help reflecting—well, isn't most cowardice senseless by its very nature?—because there were two fireproofed stairways at hand and ready to be used around opposite turns of the hall. Not only that, but anyone unselfish enough and good sport enough to remove himself so that everybody else could get down would stand a better than even chance of actually getting down ahead of them, for the elevator crawled, at best, and also had a tendency to get jammed and stick whenever it became overweighted. But I suppose it was only human nature, given the state of mass tension they were all in, for them to overlook the stairways altogether and cling to the elevator like barnacles to a waterlogged plank. No one wanted to be the one to be left behind. Everyone wanted it to be someone else.

I turned and went inside without waiting to see the outcome, for it was not an ingratiating thing to watch, and quietly closed the door after me.

It should be explained at this point that there was no possible way for me to telephone down for myself and find out just how bad the situation really was, once and for all. The hotel had been changing hands at a rate that had finally become almost annual in its frequency. Each successive management had found new and ever cleverer ways of cutting down expenses so that the profits would be that much higher. And only about six months before, the management in control had removed the phones from all the rooms, to do away with the expense of maintaining a switchboard and an operator downstairs. In its place there was just one single public coin telephone to each floor, out in the hall, and these connected only with the outside, not with the building itself. They were in a state of almost constant unusability due to mishandling.

I had heard that there was a legal action about this situation going on at the time, but in New York, as elsewhere, these things take time, and meantime the phones were out. That was the one thing sure about it all.

In short, there were only two ways for me to get any information about the fire: either at secondhand, by hearsay, as I had tried to just now from the man in the hall, or by going down in person and seeing for myself. And I had no intention of doing that and letting her remain by herself up above, even for only a few minutes time. Too much could have happened in those few minutes.

Let me be frank about it. I had not at any time from first to last any actual fear that we would both be burned alive there in the rooms. There were too many firemen running about all over the building. But death by flame comes last in most fires. Death by smoke and suffocation comes far earlier. And my own particular dread was for one that can come even earlier still: death by heart failure. Rescue was not the problem. It was concealment of any necessity for rescue that was.

I drew a glass of water, and then a second one. After emptying part of one out again, to make it seem as though that was what I had been doing all this while, taking a long, slow drink of water, I returned to the room she was in, holding one in each hand.

"I thought you might feel like having this," I said, and put one glass down next to her.

She took only a few swallows and set it aside again, while I raised my own to my mouth, but didn't take any. I wasn't sure my throat would open up to let it go down.

"I would, I feel, be untrue to the standards of the high office to which you have chosen me—" the President was saying.[5]

I gave her an elaborately skeptical look and shrugged, just to seem to be listening intently.

"You never believe them in anything they say, do you?" she chided me gently and whimsically.

"Not in politics," I admitted.

She believed me in everything—I know this for a fact—but failed to understand me in some things. Or maybe I only thought she didn't.

My first cigarette had long ago burned down past the point of being usable, so I put the tip of it out and took out another and lit that, just to give myself something to do with my hands.

They were not in the least shaky, and I was surprised to notice that. As though they were the hands of someone else. I was probably too tense and taut and tightly wound up even to be shaky. I certainly didn't feel as calm as my hands looked.

I got up again, infinitely lackadaisical, and drifted outside, carrying one of the water glasses with me as an excuse, as though to return it.

Again the leaping thrust toward the door, its quick but quiet pulling back, the worried look to see how things were going out there.

The haze in the hall, I thought, seemed a little thicker, but perhaps my fears only imagined it. There were fewer figures than the first time, that part at least was not imaginary. As though most of them had already fled to the street and safety by this time. This thought added even greater anxiety to what I was feeling already; I think it would have with anyone. No one likes the feeling of being left behind in an emergency. The hall was definitely silent, and whatever voices and noises there were, seeped into it from elsewhere, at a distance. How I longed to hear even the excited calls and scurrying feet I had the first time, as frightening as they had seemed then. This stillness was even worse.

Again I went back inside.

I still held onto the minutes before I had to tell her about it, like a miser holds onto his last few coins, because I knew once I told her, there would be no undoing it. But until I told her, nothing had yet been lost, and I couldn't bring myself to throw that advantage away, not quite yet. Her welfare depended too much on remaining unaware.

I didn't go back into the same room with her at once this time. I opened the clothes closet in the foyer, took down her winter coat, and removed it from the hanger. Even in this, circumstances favored me, for the closet in which we kept our street clothes was not in the room with her but outside, as I have just said. I had to take the coat into my own bedroom with me and lay it on the bed, for there was no other place to dispose of it without risking having her see it.

It had a silver fox collar as soft as down, and I remember running my hand over this wistfully, and hoping I wouldn't have to bundle her into it, and see her frightened pallid face looking up at me over it.

But there it lay, taken down and in readiness, in case I did have to.

Looking backward over my shoulder at it, almost the way a child does at something that he fears will jump and bite him if he takes his eyes off it for a single moment, I went back in to where she sat.

"What were you doing?" she asked me, for I'd been gone a little longer this time than the first.

"I was in my room, attending to something," I said, not quite untruthfully. "I can hear the radio from in there." Which also was no lie. I often went in there abruptly like that anyway, to jot down something for future writing before it got away from me, and then returned again just as abruptly a few minutes later. She was used to this.

She said immediately, with that ever-ready thoughtful consideration she was always so quick to show in anything that concerned me, "Well, does it interfere with whatever you're doing? Would you rather have it turned off?"

"Oh, no, no!" I quickly protested, and the thought genuinely appalled me, for to have a fire on my hands with the speech going on was bad enough, but to have a fire on my hands with no speech going on would have been even worse. It at least made it seem a little more home-like, a little more secure, more everyday-normal, to hear his voice droning on and on there throughout the rooms, if nothing else. It was comforting to hear words and phrases like "non-belligerency" and "peaceful cooperation" topping the occasional shrill upsurges of voice and occasional splatter of hastening feet outside along the hall.[6] In my gratitude I was even prepared to agree wholeheartedly with everything he said (the little of it I could gather), which would have by no means been the case without the fire to go with it.

At this point I got up and left again, for another quick inspection. Just as I got the door open, a fireman came out of the safety staircase, went loping by me around the turn of the hall, and went down it toward its far end. He was alone, but, though moving fast, not running. He had evidently come up from the floor below, to continue up here whatever it was he'd been doing down there, while perhaps somebody else took that over. I started out after him, and in this way I finally learned what the causes of the fire were and what its nature was.

On each floor there were a few small single rooms with no attached baths of their own. For the convenience of their tenants, there were two public baths on every floor. But since these were inside bathrooms, with no windows, there was an air shaft or duct behind each of them, running straight up through the building from the basement and opening out on the roof, for purposes of ventilation, and both bathrooms had a sort of square opening in the upper part of their walls with a wooden panel hinged to it, that gave onto this air shaft.

I suppose this was considered a very ingenious arrangement in the days when the hotel had first been built, but it had turned out to be an exceedingly dangerous one. People must have been throwing trash down there for years, in spite of the signs cautioning them not to, and the air shafts must not have been properly cleaned out in almost as many years. This fine night someone had at last tossed in an ill-extinguished cigarette or still glowing match-head.

So I followed the fireman, as he went down our branch of the hall. But if I were drawn after him, it was hardly in the joyous way that small boys once used to be, or were said to have been, drawn after firemen as if by magnets. There was nothing to be seen in the immediate vicinity of our own door except the lifeless-hanging haze, which now seemed to have layers of different thicknesses in it, so that it looked stratified.

"Does it look all right?" I asked him. "How does it look?" Trying not to sound as uneasy as I knew I must sound.

His answer was noncommittal. "We're doing what we can," was all he said, back over his shoulder.

I kept walking along after him, more to continue my questioning than anything else. "Do you think we ought to all get out?" I wanted to know.

"Everybody is out already," was his chilling comment.

"Well, I'm not," I couldn't help pointing out.

"Well, why aren't you?" was his only reply to that.

"Because I wasn't told to be," I argued.

But I don't think he heard me any further, because he had now reached his objective. I realized of course that he was preoccupied, and this was no time to ask him a string of questions. What I had wanted was an encouraging word, but from him I certainly didn't get it.

He went into the public bath and set to work with something that resembled a long pole-axe, jamming it down inside the chute I've already spoken of and, I think, trying to dislodge and pry off pieces of burning matter that were clinging to the brickwork lining like fungus, and must have caught fire with the heat coming up from below. I know that every time he prodded, a spurt of resentful vermillion sparks came up almost in his face, so it must have been that. It was remarkable to see how close he was standing to it, and yet how little smoke there was coming from it. Almost nothing to speak of. But I think the haze in the hall must have been slowly seeping up from the basement in some more tortuous way. What we were getting up here was only a distant offshoot of the fire. For even if there had been a strong updraft pulling the smoke through to the roof, at least a little of it would have escaped out through the open panel.

The girl who had the room diagonally across from ours on the opposite side of the hall came out and joined me as an onlooker. She was of uncertain occupation. On the other hand, the maid who cleaned her room was *very* certain what it was, and said so (though not in my mother's presence). But since they both had volatile temperaments, and had had several violent flare-ups, this might have been an uncharitable exaggeration, even if a kernel of truth did exist somewhere.

I knew only two things about her from direct observation. Every so often she dropped from sight for two or three days, and I would notice that the keyhole on the door had been plugged up, as is commonly done for nonpayment of rent. Then she would return, the plug would disappear, and conviviality (but never outright disorderliness) could be detected from within, with the sound of friends' voices, and laughter, and, I suppose, drinks.

And the second thing was that she had bought a small can of shellac or paint and coated her entire floor a glossy, shining black. The maid was the one who first told me this (her grievance was that the girl had cleaned her hands and brushes off on some of the hotel towels), and then I saw it for myself on several occasions when the door had been left ajar and I had to go by there on my errands. She was also fond of keeping a certain lamp with a dusky red shade lit, and having no other light but this. The effect of the dull red glowing on the glistening black was rather satanic, I thought. If I had been a child, I think I would have hurried past that door.

This black floor had an irritating effect on the maid, who took it as a personal affront, for some inscrutable reason. Possibly she thought it was a hint that her work was not properly done. I think it was nothing more than the very matter-of-fact and practical way the occupant took to cover up the ingrained and ineradicable grime on so many of the floors of that venerable building.

She stood looking on at the fireman with the sort of detached but fascinated interest one brings to bear on, say, workmen riveting a steel beam into place amid a shower of sparks, high up on the face of some building under construction, when one has no place else to go and nothing better to do.

She was an attractive young person, with her black hair, large dark eyes and pale beige complexion, but excruciatingly thin. She was wearing a close-fitting sweater and toreador pants, both of some vivid shade, deep orange, I think, but I can no longer be sure now. Or it might have been the reflection of the fire's sheen, playing against her and overlying some lighter color, yellow for instance, that only made it seem to be that tone. It was just an optic snapshot I had of her, in any case; I wasn't there to study costumes, at the moment.

We stood there side by side a moment, both smoking our nervous cigarettes, looking on while he chopped and prodded away at the pinpoint-corruscating brickwork down within the opening.

"I like fires," she said to me suddenly, without turning her head and continuing to watch him.

"I don't," I said grimly, and repeated it in my mind even more grimly a second time.

"Last one I was in was up in Harlem, when I was still living up there," she told me. "After it was over, me and the other people in the house and the fireman all sat down together and had a round of drinks all around."

"Are they allowed to do that, firemen?" I asked uncertainly.

"It was Christmas Eve," she explained. "This was a Christmas-tree fire."

"Oh," I said, digesting the unfamiliar ethics of this.

A sudden upsurge of angrily molested sparks drove him back almost on top of us, and drove us back in turn to escape being trodden on, so the conversation was broken off.

With that, she suddenly seemed to lose all further interest, as if she had expected something far more dramatic than this pedestrian hacking and chipping. She turned and walked away along the hall, and went back into her own room, I suppose to resume whatever contemplations the black floor and red lamp furnished her with, now that this momentary diversion had palled.[7]

I decided it was high time for me to get back where I belonged, too. But as I backed out of the bath doorway in which I had been standing watching, a heavily built, languid, slow-walking, slow-talking woman, whom I knew to be a floor neighbor, came out into the hall, at the end opposite from the girl, where her own room lay, and stood there looking at me with a sort of mute supplication. Or so I translated it, anyway. As a matter of fact, even on normal occasions she usually presented a woebegone appearance, walked at a trailing shuffle, and was almost continuously under the influence of alcohol. Since she had two small children and regularly received a relief allotment for their maintenance (a large part of which was unquestionably diverted toward alcohol), this behavior could not be considered commendable.

Still, paradoxically enough, she was what I would call a good mother, as against many a more sober but more severe parent. She did not neglect them; they were at all times kept neat and properly dressed, and she never even scolded, much less struck or shouted at them, as far as I ever witnessed. I suppose this was attributable to her own befogged and supine temperament. The main thing is they gave every indication of being happy children, and I imagine, since they had never seen her in any other condition but her habitual one, they thought it was the normal one for her to be in, and didn't know the difference. In some instances, I think, the children of the bottle, as I call them, can be quite as happy as others.

Only a short while before the night of this fire, I recall, she had stopped me in the hall one day, and at great length, ramblingly, and almost unintelligibly, she put some sort of complicated question to me, holding onto my coat lapel and teetering, in the meantime, as she usually did when speaking to anyone. I finally made it out to be this: could she have milk delivered right to her door, as she had seen me have done, and if so, how did she go about it? I told her of course she could, anyone could, all she had to do was make the arrangement with the deliveryman.

When I opened my door the next night to take in the milk, after I'd heard it set down outside, I was just in time to overhear a low-voiced, querulous, and interminable argument going on between the two of them, the milkman and herself, down at the end of the hall in front of her door. He finally broke it off short by turning his back on her and walking away. When he passed by me, I asked him what the trouble had been.

"She wants the milk on credit, like you get yours," he said sulkily. "I told her new customers have to pay me cash on the spot."

"Ah, let her have it," I remonstrated. "She has two kids. If she doesn't give you your money, I'll make good for it."

I closed the door and went in again.

Two nights later, when he again came around to leave my own modest unvarying order, I noticed standing on the floor to one side of him one of those large wire-wickered carrier baskets they use when they have an unusually heavy delivery to bring into a building. It had about eight or ten compartments in it, and every one of them was filled with a bottle or carton. Not only milk, which would have been plausible enough, but all its ramified by-products, and many that weren't, as well: orange drink, chocolate-flavored drink, buttermilk, yogurt, even ready-made eggnog.

There wasn't a liquid product of this dairy company, one of the largest in the New York metropolitan area, which had been omitted.

This didn't register on my mind in time, the first time I saw it, and I simply closed the door again.

But when, upon the next delivery, the carrier basket again stood there, stacked to overflowing as before, I asked him whom this giant consignment was for.

"Down there, at the end of the hall," he said, pitching his thumb backward.

A sudden suspicion entered my head. "Is she paying for all this?" I asked him.

"Why, no," he told me. "She seems to think you are."

Regretfully but firmly I had to decline then and there to sponsor any more of these proxy deliveries, although I allowed the one he had on hand to proceed unhampered. Still, I didn't blame her in the least for the attempt, and it was certainly impossible to resent it. It would have been a little like resenting a lumbering mother-bear because she paws at honey to give her cubs.

She stood there now at the end of the hall, seeming even wider than she actually was as the thin haze soft-focused her outlines and made them seem to quiver. It even made her eyes seem rounder and whiter as they loomed through it like those of a perplexed calf.

"Mister," she said plaintively.

The majority of the hotel tenants, herself included, were Negro. My mother and I were the only exceptions on our own particular floor. At the time we had first moved in, with scarcely a dollar to spare, and with the Great Depression of the Thirties dropping steadily downward to what seemed bottomless depths, it had been a shabby, genteel, and (most important) inexpensive "family hotel," as the designation then was. By the time my affairs were in better shape, it was already a home to us, we were used to it, and I felt with all a writer's typical superstition that it had brought me luck and it would have been ungrateful of me to move. Meanwhile, as the concentration camp of Harlem burst apart its barbed-wire boundaries, and as the new mores began to convert the general population, and more and more doors began to open all over the city, the composition of the locality immediately surrounding us, which was upper West Side New York, had altered to a marked extent.

I put this observation in only for the sake of making this episode I am describing as literal as possible. The classification is quite immaterial in itself. I was never conscious of any difference, nor did I ever receive the slightest indication from anyone else that they were either. We were all just people together. Some poor, some better off than that; some young, some older than that; some healthy, some (like my mother) sick almost unto death.

"Mister," she said now, standing there mezzotinted by the stagnant stripes of haze.

"What is it?" I said warily, determined not to let myself become enmeshed now of all times in one of those interminable hallway apocryphals of hers, from which I usually had to detach myself by edging away from her backwards step by step, even on more expendable occasions.

"Can you come here a minnut?"

"Not now," I said. "I've got to go back inside here."

"Please, mister," she wheedled. "Oeny for just a minnut. I want to show you something."

She looked so helpless standing there, and so fatuous—well, I went, wondering what *I* could do to help her. I needed to be helped myself.

As soon as she saw that I was actually coming, she went back inside her room without waiting for me to reach it. The pitiful little room was not even directly on the hallway itself but pushed back from it at the end of a little inlet or secondary passage. It had a window looking out on the grimness of an opposite court-wall, but one entire side of it was backed against the very air shaft that the fireman around on the other side was at that moment trying so hard to rid of its clambering, tendril-like flames. Not only that, there was the same cupboard-like panel high up on its wall, just as in the bathroom, and hers stood open. In the opening you could see the stringy flames wavering listlessly like tangled skeins of orange yarn, as though somebody unseen in there just up above the orifice were busily knitting with them.

She was standing back in the center of the room again now, where she must have been standing previously, mesmerized by it as a focal point ever since she had first opened the wall panel and discovered it, interrupting herself only long enough to waver out into the hall to look for a word of reassurance or encouragement above this phenomenon of an intoxicated world. The two lovely little children were pressed against her, one on each side, and she had a hand on top of each one's head, but whether to safeguard them or to fortify her own fluctuating equilibrium it would not have been possible to say. At least they were not frightened or crying, that much I was relieved to see. Perhaps—no, undoubtedly—her own blurred, reality-insulated attitude conditioned theirs, so from that point of view it was all to the good, at least. As I recall, the smaller one had a finger hooked into its mouth, while the larger one stared with the round, wondering (but unwavering) eyes with which childhood meets so many of the unfathomable crises of the grown-up universe.

But in order to give the situation its true perspective, there are these favorable circumstances to be mentioned: the window was shut, so there was no out-draft to pull the flames through into the room itself. It was a wall fire, feeding on the webs of dust wool and other matter clinging to the brickwork facing of the chute, and not flaring out widely. It gave off no heat, it gave off no smoke. Or if it did, they were both funneled upward and out through the roof. In short, if there is such a thing, it was a visual fire rather than a tactile one.

And yet, of course, when all that has been said, the fact still remains that she was standing with her two children within a small room, not more than eight or ten feet away from naked flame with no barrier before it.

The first thing she did was point accusingly. "Look," she pouted, heavy-lipped.

"I see it," I said shortly. "Why do you stand here like this?"

"I don't know what to do," she said vaguely.

"Where's your husband?" I asked her.

"He's away," she said. "He work' for the railroad."

I had heard that: that he was a pullman-car porter.

"Don't you think it would be better to take them downstairs with you and wait outside?"

She shook her head distressedly. "I can't *do* that. Every time I take them out on the street with me, they get away from me."

"Can't you hold onto them by the hand?"

"If I hold onto one, then the other get' away. If I go to get that one, then the one I got get' away."

I didn't pursue this any further. I couldn't compel her to leave if she didn't want to.

"Why do you let it stay open like that?" I said almost irritably. I edged up to it from the side to keep from getting scorched and tried closing it by giving it a push, but it came right back again each time. One of the hinges must have been sprung.

"I heard some kind of noise in there and I open' it to see," she told me. "I thought it was mice. We gets mice in there sometimes."

She eyed the grinning, teeth-like little flame tips reproachfully. "I'm nervous," she said mournfully. "I can't help it. Things like that just make me nervous, that's all."

"So am I nervous," I said, to reassure her. "You're not the only one. Anyone would be."

Then I said, "If you won't go downstairs with them, why don't you at least go and stand in the open doorway over there, instead of staying out in the middle of the room like that. It may shoot out unexpectedly and singe you. This way you can get down the hall and out if you have to."

She did so, but she still kept saying, "I'm nervous."

At the time I couldn't see anything funny in it, I was under too much pressure to have a normal sense of proportion myself, but when I recalled it to mind the next day, the ludicrousness of the understatement struck me with full impact. Live flame tips jittering up and down in full view within the exposed chute only a few feet away from her, and, as though she were admitting some minor defect of character, some flaw, which the merest of trifles could bring out, and which therefore ought to be apologized for: "Things like that make me nervous. I can't help it, they just make me nervous, that's all."

I left her and went back to my own home.

"The present moment is a grave one, but we are hopeful that reason and right will prevail—"[8]

A different world swept around me with the closing of the door, as though a heavy, muffling felt curtain had dropped. A half-forgotten world of normalcy from far back—was it an hour ago?—was it days ago? It felt more like a lifetime ago.

I made my token payment to the figment of a continuous, uninterrupted presence within the apartment. I don't remember what I said. Or if I said anything. Probably the President said it for me, and far better than I could. Then I immediately went out of the room again. I'd seen something just now, on my way in, or thought I had, which I didn't like the looks of. I wanted to see if I'd been right about it. I looked a second time, and saw that I had been right, and the breath that I slowly drew in felt cold going down, just like menthol. For, around the seams of the front door the smoke-haze was now beginning to float in, compressed by the unevenness of the frame (the woodwork was old) into multiple fine filaments, like stirring willow fronds or rippling threads of silken fringe. I say that about it now, but I didn't think that about it then. It gave me too much apprehension for me to give it pretty names.

You couldn't see it at all if you stared at it frontally, it was still too transparent. But if you slanted yourself over to one side and pinpointed it against some darker surface (as I did now), you could see the darker surface fade a little, as though a thin film of ashes had paled its color, and quiver a little, as though heat were creating a light refraction in the air. This was far more visible along the top than lower down; I suppose smoke in its infiltrations always is.

It was only beginning in a small way, but everything begins in a small way, I didn't have to remind myself, and once begun, what way was there to stop it?[9] I wondered why it had taken so long to penetrate, at that. The hall outside had been like a shadowy steambath for a long time past. I supposed, though, it had only now reached a sufficient density out there to force its way through seams and cracks and whatever other vents there were.

I remembered an electric fan I'd bought the summer before, to make her more comfortable. I opened the storage closet and found it on the shelf, where I'd put it when the hot weather was over. It was small, with rubber wings that slightly curled over at their top edges, but at least it had the virtue of slowly swinging from one side to the other and back again every few revolutions. I planted it on the floor and aimed it so that its radius covered both the crack underneath the door and the two seams that ran up along its sides. Then I plugged it into the nearest baseboard outlet. Immediately it blurred into motion with dogged industriousness, and the gauzy wisps all disappeared, like grayish-blue pollen blown into dissolution.

It was such a small fan, though, sitting there huddled like a little green grasshopper with legs tucked under it, and there was so much haze for it to blow away, whole hallways full, a whole building full. Then when I looked up above, I saw that it wasn't succeeding anyway. The ceiling was beginning to get fuzzy. Its appearance was like that of a crystal-clear pond bottom when sun-shadows flicker across it. The sort of shadows that cast no shadow of their own, only mottle the top of the water. I knew why that was. The fan's breath couldn't reach up that high. There was a flanged screw yoking it at the neck, and it couldn't elevate above a certain angle.

Inside in the other room, I heard my mother give a low-voiced cough, and then it was repeated twice more, each time more strenuously than before.

It has started, I said to myself.

I stopped all further thought of mechanical make shifts then and there, and decided the time had come to get human help, and get her out of there fast, while I still could. And if I still could. There was only one person in the hotel to turn to for that help, who would give it to me if he could, I knew. And that was Joe.

Joe had first made his appearance at the hotel in the capacity of a desk clerk, one of a long, kaleidoscopic succession who changed more frequently even than the managements. He didn't last long, any more than any of the others had before him. But in Joe's case there was this difference: part of the original arrangement had been that Joe be given a room in the hotel, which was carried out as agreed. Then when he gave up his desk job, or was himself given up (depending upon which side you heard it from), he stayed on in the room anyway. He didn't pay rent for it as others did. He just remained in status quo. Every so often the management would recall his continuing presence, most likely because they happened to see him as he passed in or out, and would angrily threaten to put him out, and even tell him to his face to go. But somehow they never did, and Joe continued to come and go imperturbably, and take his ease upon the steps outside the entrance and bid all comers the time of day.

I think one obstacle, though hardly an insuperable one, that may have kept the management from carrying out their oft-repeated and as often postponed threats to put him out was the fact that Joe, alone of anyone else in the hotel, had fastened a padlock to his room door. It would have been the work of only a minute for the house mechanic to have sundered it, but he was overworked and much in demand, and the minute never seemed to come.[10] When the management was hot to have Joe out, the mechanic was busy on some emergency elsewhere and couldn't be called away. When the mechanic at last had the minute to spare, the management had cooled again and forgot to give him the order. I know this strains belief, but it was actually the haphazard way in which the hotel was run.

As for the padlock, Joe never said why. It might have been to guard against robbery, of which there had been a countless number of cases in the hotel of late years. Or it might just as readily have been to guard against the, let's say, end results of robbery. I know this may sound unfair toward a one-time well-liked acquaintance, but it was Joe himself who once referred in passing to having had what he termed a "run-in" with the police some years before. He never told me what about, and I didn't want to know. But judging Joe simply from knowing him, I feel sure it could not have been a wholly indefensible case. The laws of property are not always infallible. And he had been only eighteen then, I think he said.

I liked Joe, though our contacts were limited to random chats on the entrance steps of the hotel and the once or twice that he'd accompanied me companionably for a block or two on my way toward some destination. And Joe seemed to like me too, though he showed it only by inference and indirection (which is the only palatable way it can be shown). One time, for instance, I happened to mention in passing that the lamp by which I did my writing was no longer in first-class working order. Joe didn't seem to notice the remark, or if he did, made no comment. But a few days later, when I answered a knock at the door, there he stood without any warning, holding in both hands a handsome green-shaded lamp with expensive brass fittings, which certainly was far above the average of most of the lamps to be met with in the other rooms around us in the hotel. Whether it was hotel property or not I was unable to determine, and didn't have the ungraciousness to ask him.

Without a word he held it out to me, put a finger alongside his mouth to indicate silence (the hotel maid happened to be in my rooms at the time), and winked to indicate mutual understanding. Then he turned around and walked off again as unexpectedly as he had showed up.

But, since he was not working behind the desk any more by that time, I can only assume (if it was hotel property at all) that he had retained the official pass key from his desk-clerk days, used it to enter some apartment that he happened to know was between occupancies, and withdrawn the lamp, all for my sake, whom I suppose he thought of as a creative person and therefore entitled to any such benefits by that very fact alone.

In that case it could not have been called a theft, since he didn't profit by it himself but passed it on to me, a lawful tenant of the hotel; but it was certainly an unauthorized removal or transfer. Nevertheless I accepted it in the spirit in which it was offered, an act of altruism and good fellowship, with no self-interest attached whatever.

I wanted to show my appreciation in some tangible form, but I didn't want to offer him a tip, as one would a bellboy. I had already detected a considerable amount of very prickly personal pride in Joe. He neither smoked nor drank, so I couldn't offer him a gift in either one of those categories. Accordingly, the next time I saw him I handed him a book in which I had written on the fly-leaf, and also winked, as he had done, to show him what it was meant to be in appreciation of. He seemed to like that very much.

I wish that I could remember his last name. I had great difficulty hanging onto it even at the time, and now it's gone for good. It wasn't that it was too long or difficult or grotesque. It was an Italian name, and I think the trouble was that. Joe was the most un-Italian-looking Italian I have ever seen. Slow-moving, stolid, phlegmatic of speech and lacking in hand gestures, with his beech-bark tan hair and hazel eyes, he looked a typical Hollander or Swede. (Only, there is no such thing as a typical anything, of course; what I mean is the popular conception of what one looks like.) His name just didn't seem to go with him, to fit him properly, the way some names do their owners. He must have been the offspring of a mixed marriage, the name the only thing he'd inherited of his father's. But just Joe is enough, no last name needed: one of the nicer people of this world.

Now the time had come for me to call on him for help. And I knew that it wouldn't be refused.

His room was down on the third, and to get to it as quickly as possible, I didn't bother with the elevator, overworked and loaded with escapees as I had last seen it to be. I pulled open one of the two flap-doors sealing off the nearest safety staircase, and went charging down at headlong speed. This was nothing to be done with impunity. On every landing was a fixture without an electric light bulb. They had all been stolen off the walls. It was like running inside a box in the dark. The feeling of gravity told you you must be going down, but your other senses couldn't confirm it.

The sensation was incomplete, but the hazards weren't. There were fruit peels on those steps to make your foot skid and fly off into space. There were discarded newspaper pages lying there, to conceal where the rim of the step ended and the drop began, and send you crashing if you should overreach it. There were cartons of refuse imperfectly pushed back against the wall to stub your toe or nick your ankle against, and be thrown off balance by. A beer can might roll harmlessly out from under you, if you were lucky and didn't pin it down squarely with the flat of your foot and be semi-somersaulted as if by ball-bearing action. At the turns there were no level spaces, as on most staircases, to prop your equilibrium against for a moment as you rounded them. On their inner side the steps were telescoped like the gathered sticks of a fan, so compressed they could barely take the back half of the heel. And on their outer side they were so expanded they made you lose precious time making the lengthier circuit of them. Besides, the sudden decrease in frequency of step-count was an added risk in itself, throwing you off beat and making your step short and totter.

The only light on them all the way down was a faint greenish, fishtank pallor that came peering in at each floor through the thick, wire-meshed rippled glass panels set into the upper halves of the fire doors, and its radius was so restricted it didn't touch the stairs at all, just cast a little gauzy patch on the floor directly underneath where it entered.

Even though I didn't see most of this now, I knew all these things from other, more leisurely and much more prudent progresses up or down, with a match or a pocket flash, at times when the elevator was stuck, or a master fuse had blown and all the current in the building was off.

But somehow, in spite of all the treacheries to be met with on the way down, I was still upright on both feet when I reached the third floor (identifying it by count only) and shoved open the safety doors. I don't think even a headlong fall would have been enough to stop me, not unless I received a knock on the head along with it. When you're doing something for your own sake, you take account of such things; when you're doing it for someone else's sake, you don't.

The hall down here was as deserted as the one up on my own floor. Everyone seemed to have fled the building. Whether it had more haze in it, or less, I have no clear recollection. My whole attention was centered on Joe's door as I headed down toward it at a run, the way you fix your eyes on the concentric circles of a target. I could see the padlock on it even before I got there. But it was only when I stopped short in front of it, and already had my hand up to the knocker, that I saw the thing about it that really mattered: it was clasped about both loops at once, not just hanging idly from one. It was locked from the outside, would have to be, to be in that position.

I knew by that. No Joe. He'd gone, he wasn't in there.

But I went ahead and knocked anyway. The urge to knock was too strong, I guess, to be deflected on the instant like that. I did all the redundant things that you do when a door that you desperately want to be opened, isn't opened; even though you know it can't be opened, for there's no one there to do it. Tripped the knocker, rapped with my knuckles, low and hurriedly, worried the knob. All reflex actions, purely and simply, outliving my disappointment by a moment or two and trying in that way to reverse it.

Then I just stood there, quite still, holding the back of my hand to my forehead.

This probably was the low point of the whole shriveling experience, the worst few moments of that livid evening. No Joe to help me with her, give me a hand. Gone from his room to a safer place, like all the rest of them. And I had to have help, couldn't manage it by myself. It was a physical impossibility, that was my whole problem. Years of night work, fission-like smoking, scanty sleep and sketchy feeding, had kept me thin and underweight as an adolescent who has overnight attained his full height.[11] Many thin people have considerable reserves of strength, it is true. So did I, for that matter; I must have had, to have lived such a life for so long, but mine was all constitutional, not muscular. I knew, by one or two attempts I'd made to lift her into bed during the earlier part of her illness, that I could not support her full weight in my arms, slight as it was, for any length of time. I would have staggered a few steps and then toppled with her or, worse still, dropped her injuriously. I was even then carrying around on me an unprotected and un-operated-on lesion that must have originated at that former time.[12]

This was the whole reason for my seeking out Joe, this and nothing else. Not cowardice, not need of moral support, but sheer impotency.

I turned and went away from his door. I tried to think of improvisations that might make up for the strength I didn't have and the help I couldn't get. Shuffling her out before me seated on a chair, or drawing her after me on it in reverse. But that would have been too bumpy to be altogether successful, and even if it hadn't been, there was something ignominious about it. She shouldn't have to pay for safety with her dignity; I valued that too much, and had always respected it too highly, to let anything impair it, even at a time like this. I discarded the half-formed notion of the chair as quickly as it had entered my mind.

The firemen were my obvious recourse, but every time I sighted one in the distance—and they always seemed to be in the distance, just going away from me around a turn or off in another direction—and hailed him to try to make my dilemma known, I either got no sign he heard or got no answer. They were all too busy with the sum-total of the emergency to be able to stop for any isolated instances of it. That was natural, I suppose, but it was no solace to me.

I had to go back up the inky stairs I'd just come down, couldn't stay there waiting for help that wasn't to be had. I sprinted up them at least as fast as I'd made the trip the other way, but the going was twice as hard. Scissoring my legs as widely apart as I could, to take in three and four steps at a time between them, I remember thinking fleetingly I ought to be grateful and not rueful that there was so little in weight and so little of girth for them to carry. They might for all purposes have been detached legs without a body, going up by themselves, like in those trick, double-exposure "supernatural" films you used to see, for all the bulk they had to carry on top of them. The advantage my lack of poundage gave me running up those stairs right then more than compensated for any sheepish embarrassment I had ever felt about it.

I got back up to my own floor, matchlessly fast but half strangled.

I went inside again, where the President's voice still dwelled on the unmolested air, and there was a sort of blissful unawareness still tenuously intact, though fragile and precarious as a soap bubble surrounded by a thousand pointing pins.

And to keep it as it was, when I was back in the room with her, I held my breath altogether at first, then let it out surreptitiously a little at a time, then drew a new one in in the same constrained way, all to quell the heavy rise and fall of my rib cage and keep it below the point of notice.

"You're in and out, in and out, the whole time," my mother remarked during a Presidential paragraph break.

I turned one hand idly over on its back. "It's nothing," I said. "I get these restless evenings. You've seen them before."

In a minute or two the breathlessness was over, and the hectic stair descent and climb back were just as though they'd never been. And for all the good they'd done, I couldn't help reflecting dismally, they might just as well *not* have ever been.

Now as I sat there crouched forward above my own lap, hands loosely dangling before me, I seemed to be deeply intent on every word he was saying, but what I was actually doing was watching with my mind's eye the minutes go by like separate little entities, like beads coursing down a tilted spillway, waiting to pounce on a certain still unidentifiable one as it came along, and lift my head and say to her at long last:

"Now don't be frightened, but there's something that I want to tell you..."

Then as I waited for it, this indicated moment, not knowing how I'd know it when it came, only that I would, the thought occurred to me: "I'll look once more from the window. Just once more, before I say it. One added minute can't make that much difference, either way." I straightened up, put my hands to the arms of the chair, and got to my feet. At the same time I couldn't help admitting to myself, What was the good? What could I hope to find, except that it had gotten worse? Such things don't stand still, remain as they were indefinitely.

I left her and went out of the room once more. In the front room, I went over to the window. As I took hold of it by the finger grooves and it went up before me, along with the inrushing night cold came a feeling of sickening dismay that almost made me not want to look. The noise out there was on the upswing again, seemed louder than it had been up until just now. Again there were restless intermittent bells clamoring, as there hadn't been since the first onrushing, feverish arrival back at the beginning. And the heavy motors seemed to be pounding more deeply so that even the glass in the pane over my head vibrated and buzzed, and not just purring quiescently with only force enough to pump the water, as they had been doing all this while.

The rhythm of their presence had changed again, and it was faster, louder, more crescendo in every way.

I bent over acutely and looked down. You had to, or the ledge cut perspective off short; it was wide as a shelf. And then I saw what was taking place.

"And then I saw"—those words can tell you what I did see, they cannot tell what I felt. I often think that feelings can't be transcribed, anyway. Feelings can only be *felt*, they can never be worded. When you say, "I am happy," you are not describing what happiness really is. When you say, "I am overcome with relief," you are not telling what that is either. Feelings are a thing apart, not of the spoken speech or the written word, and they cannot be transferred to either one.

An endlessly elongated hook-and-ladder apparatus (which hadn't been used anyway, from first to last) was moving, was clumsily maneuvering, to extricate itself from the jammed-up mass of other vehicles and leave the scene.

It was the first break in their ranks. It was the only one underway, so far. All the rest stood immovable, none of them stirred; but I knew the fire had been beaten, its back had been broken, or nothing would have left there at all. The rest would just be downgrade from now on, the checking up, the exhaustive security measures, to make sure no danger remained. Many a fire left for dead has come back to life again with sharper fangs than ever.

Even the crowd had very much melted away, only a few die-hards still lingered on. And the mass instinct of the crowd can be relied on, it always knows when a climax is past.

I was happy. I was overcome with relief.

After awhile I drew my head in. When I went around to the foyer the little fan was still whirring away valiantly—but with nothing to overcome any more. I opened the door and looked out. The haze had almost all cleared away. Just a trace of it remained here and there, where the electric lights were, like spiderwebs clinging around them.

The fireman who'd done battle beside the blazing bathroom chute was gone. From behind the closed door of the girl with the black floor came the low-voiced moaning of a lonely blues. That, and the pungent odor of some kind of weed. No one else had come back to their rooms yet. There wasn't a soul in sight. The hall stretched wide and empty before me. What a beautiful hall. It had never struck me before what a beautiful hall we had. So straight, so peaceful and crystal clear in aspect.

I felt good will toward the whole world. I felt drained of energy, but at peace. I turned and went in, and softly closed the door.

The little fan still squatted there low, battling away like a pugnacious bantam. I tugged its plug out of the outlet, and there was a pinhead blue spark. Then the fan slowly laid down its arms. I picked it up (almost tenderly) and put it aside somewhere.

It had grown quiet in here now too. I noticed that for the first time.

"You have just heard the President of the United States," I heard a solitary voice say.

Then the national anthem began its slow, stately cadences.

When I went back into the room, my mother turned her head and gave me an inquiring look. "What did you think of it?"

"Well," I said, and quite truthfully, "for one thing, it seemed almost unendurably long."

I turned the knob and shut it off.

Then I said another thing that was equally true. "I don't think I ever want to hear him speak again."

She smiled deprecatingly.

The speech was over. The time had now come for her to retire. Before she retired each night, at the doctor's suggestion, I always brought in a cup of slightly warmed milk to her. Often I had to coax her to take it, so in order to encourage her and keep her company I'd fallen into the habit of joining her in a cup myself, although to tell the truth, of all the things in this world there's nothing I've always hated more than the taste and scent of milk.

But tonight I felt played out and needed a little bracing up, so I brought myself in instead a little pony glass of Three-Star Hennessy and joined her with that.

She looked at it, then she said to me with a question in her voice, "You never do that."

I decided I might as well tell her. It was over now. And she would only hear it the next day from the maid, with many frightening details added, if I didn't. So I said as casually as I could, "We had a little trouble here tonight. We had a little fire here."

"I know we did," she replied at once. "I knew all along."

I was almost speechless. "You knew, and yet you sat there quietly listening...!"

"I could tell by your face how worried you were," she said with the utmost simplicity. "I thought it would only make you worry more, if you knew that I knew."

There was nothing I could say to her. I simply reached out and covered her small pale hand with my own.

She is gone now, but whenever I hear the word *courage*, I think of her and I think of that night.

V
The Maid Who Played the Races

Set sometime during the 1960s, the fifth and final chapter of Blues
of a Lifetime *portrays Woolrich alone, on vacation in a Seattle hotel
room where, as his title explains, he met "The Maid Who Played the
Races." One of the hotel maids, misunderstanding a conversation with
Woolrich, had thought his occupation to be "rider" and not "writer."
In other words, she believed Woolrich was a jockey at the horse races.
Eagerly soliciting his racetrack advice—which Woolrich wryly provides
her, cruelly failing to confess to the joke—she places her next bet
accordingly. What follows is a humorous tale that hardly resembles the
somber tones of previous chapters.*

*In the last line of the autobiography, after Woolrich's racetrack tips
have begun to falter, he leaves the hotel alone, but unburdened. As in
most of Woolrich's lighter short stories, a somber undercurrent flows
beneath the* joie de vivre *percolating along the surface of his prose. "The
Maid Who Played the Races," as it concludes these "blues" of a lifetime,
leaves readers with a memorable image of Woolrich facing anonymity
(a metaphor for death?) with both courage and humor.*

People who live transiently in hotels seldom see the maids who
clean and make up their rooms for them. If at all possible, this is tactfully
done while the tenants are out. They quit the room in the morning
leaving a disheveled bed, a bathroomful of wilted towels, and all the
rest, and when they come back later on in the day, they unlock their
door to a room as trim and fresh and attractively well ordered as it was
at the time they were first shown into it. Unseen hands do this, and
they, the occupants, never even think twice about it. It is part of what
they paid for when they purchased the room.

And I have never been any exception to the rule myself. I have lived
in many a hotel room for days, for weeks even, and left without ever
seeing who it was who daily placed those fresh little cakes of wrapped
soap on the shelf over the washstand, or inserted new little books of
matches into the niches of the ashtray, or even meticulously put down
a dime (which must have fallen out of my pocket and lain unnoticed
on the floor) on the edge of the night stand where it could not fail
to be seen and repossessed.

Once in a while at the end of a long corridor or going just around a turn I have glimpsed some shadowy, soft-moving female figure whose light-colored unadorned smock and lack of street clothes told me she must be one of these phantom-like creatures. And once in a while I have seen a tiered conveyance, a sort of wheeled pushcart, standing motionless before some partly open door, its various compartments stacked with freshly folded linen, stationery, sterilized glasses encased in cellophane, and all the other multiplicity of things that go into a hotel room, and known that one of them, unseen as ever, must be busy in there at the time.

And when my stay came to an end, I'd place my modest but grateful tip on the dresser top, or hand it over in an envelope at the desk downstairs, just as superstitious savages used to place offerings in certain indicated spots meant for spirits whom they had never seen and never expected to see but whom they wished to show appreciation to nevertheless, and I'd go my way still without ever having seen her, this kindly servitor, from first to last.

But one day, while I was staying at the Roosevelt Hotel in Seattle,[1] I returned to my room unexpectedly for something that I had forgotten to take with me when I left it the first time. The door was ajar when I came to it, so I knew that the maid was busy in it. I widened it and stepped inside, and came face to face with a bustling, alert little old lady hopping about in there like a sparrow. At first glance she looked to me to be about seventy, but if not that, must have been at the least well into her sixties. Possibly it was the unexpectedness of seeing anyone that old in the first place that made her seem even older.

My first reaction was surprise that they would hire anyone that age for the work, which is hours long, repetitious and tiring after all. My second was a feeling of pity for her, at having to work at all at such an age, or—since I dislike the word *pity*, which to my mind has a connotation of superiority—a feeling of sympathy, let's say.

Neither feeling lasted very long. Neither one was called for.

She was competent and deft enough, as far as that went. But more important, there was a vivacity about her, a cheerfulness, which showed she wasn't having a bad time of it at all. Every move she made was quick and agile. She acted as though the work were no task to her, as though she were so habituated to it she never gave it a thought, even actually enjoyed it. And when someone acts as if they enjoy something, you can usually count on it they do.

She might have already progressed a considerable distance through this world and toward the next, but she was still very much of this one, every crackling inch of her. One only had to look at her to see that. The only thing about her that showed weathering was her face.

It was like a mask of an old face put onto some elfin, ageless body. And even it was only old in texture, not in animation.

We said hello to one another. Then she said, cocking a reassuring finger upright, "I'm just finishing up. I'll bring you your towels, and I'll be all through."

"That's all right," I said, "don't hurry on my account."

When she came back with the towels, she asked me if I were checking out.

"No," I said, "I'm staying for some time yet. Maybe several weeks. I'm not sure."

"Fine," she said approvingly. "Good. That's nice."

I don't know whether the length of such a stay was a little out of the usual (I learned later that they had a rather rapid turnover at that hotel because of the airport traffic), or whether it was just her own curiosity that prompted her, but the next thing she wanted to know was, "Do you mind my asking what you do?"

"I'm a writer," I said.

This time she was unmistakably overjoyed. Although she didn't actually clap her hands together, her whole attitude indicated that gesture of exultation.

"Oh!" she cried, "then maybe you can give me some tips!"

I didn't quite follow this, although I felt sure that she didn't mean money—tips, gratuities. In the first place, no hotel worker would ask outright for such a thing; they don't have to. It is taken for granted, it is expected, customary. And secondly, even if it had been permissible, she didn't strike me as the type who would do so. I didn't detect any of the hardness, the calculation, about her that would prompt it.

"Tips?" I said blankly. "What kind of tips?"

"Tips on the horses," she chattered. "At Longacres.[2] You must know. You're on the inside."

I grinned, still as uncomprehending as ever. I'd heard of Longacres, which I knew to be the local Seattle racetrack, although I had never been out there at the time. "What makes you think I know anything about the horses?"

"Well, if you ride them, you must know," she insisted.

Now I finally thought I understood. In fact I knew I did. We all of us alike speak English in this country, and we all understand each other without too much difficulty. Still it must be admitted there are local variations by the score, mainly in the matter of tempo and syllabic emphasis, particularly at such a distance as from one coast to the other. I had heard my own specific brand of speech, which I had always prided myself was absolutely colorless, referred to on several occasions as a "New York brogue" (a thing which I never knew existed until then). Out here in the Northwest, the speech is far slower, and comes out thinner and clearer, which I mean higher in pitch and less throaty. And therefore less prone to being misunderstood.

And after all, of the five sounds in each of the two words that had caused the confusion between us, *writer* and *rider*, the "d" and "t" are the only ones that are dissimilar. And even they can sound alike if spoken carelessly or slurred.

She thought I was a jockey.

And, naturally enough, she wanted to benefit all she could by this happy and unlooked-for juxtaposition, which might never occur again in the ordinary course of events. She dropped her voice to a conspiratorial whisper and asked, "Aren't you allowed to? Is it against the law?" And before I could answer that, which as a matter of fact I couldn't, for I knew absolutely nothing about it one way or the other, she went on wheedlingly, "I'll keep it to myself. I won't pass it on to anyone else."

I don't know why I didn't clear up the misunderstanding then and there. A word would have been enough, just as a word had caused it in the first place. I think I must have been secretly flattered at being mistaken for a racehorse rider, one of those small but wiry men who crouch low over their mount's neck and fly down the stretch at breakneck speed and sometimes take a spill.

All my life long I've admired the active and physically competitive callings and wished that I had been equipped by nature to take up one of them instead of entering into the one that did come to me. Not the poet in his ivory tower nor the painter at his easel nor the business executive at his desk—none of that—but the bantamweight in the ring (which was the heaviest class even my most unbridled daydreams dared to conjure up for me) or the racecar driver or the pilot (1930 vintage, when to "solo flight" the ocean meant a headline all over the world) or the swift-turning hockey player sending up snow sprays of shaved ice—those were the things that, if I'd had it over again, I'd have wanted for myself. Not to win at it, necessarily, just to do it. I used to say to myself, in my early days before the mold had hardened about me, "You only live it once, so why not live it as a man, not as a mole?"

So, it wasn't that I wanted to impress this elderly chambermaid. Who cared about that? She'd leave the room in a moment. No doubt I would never see her again, just as I'd never seen her before in all the time I'd already been there. It was myself that I wanted to impress, I think, far more.

I thought: let me feel big for a moment or two, let me feel good, let me glow. Let me feel like someone who does something for a change. Let me feel like the sort of a man I used to think when I was a boy I was surely going to turn into some day. What harm is there? And how often do I have the chance? How often have I ever been taken for a bike racer or coxswain or a racing crewman—or a jockey? How often will I be again? Enjoy it for a second.

Any pleasure I ever got from my writing was never pleasure as a *man*. I don't know if I can make this clear or not. What got the pleasure was a selfless thing, a shadowy thing, a bloodless, bodiless hand poised over a row of typewriter keys. But to be mistaken for a jockey for a moment, that was pleasure as a *man*.

"I haven't got a scratch sheet handy," I said, to put her off.

It occurred to me afterwards, not right as I said it, that a real jockey would probably have known the names of the entries by heart, without needing to consult a scratch sheet. But neither did this seem to occur to her, or if it did, she may have thought it was just a lame excuse, an evasion on my part, to get out of giving her the information she was so anxious to have.

In any case, she didn't importune me any further, but gave me a little subdued nod of parting, and went out and softly closed the door after her. Her face, I thought, the last glimpse of it I had as she did this, had a crestfallen cast to it, but it might not have been that so much as simply the changeover from the animation that had so steadily ignited it the whole time she was in my presence. It is rather senseless to show animation to an empty hallway; there is nothing there to bring it about.

I shrugged, and chuckled slightly to myself, and thought that was about the end of it.

But in a matter of minutes, before I'd had a chance to leave the room once more myself, there was a sly little tap at the door, and when I went over to it and opened it, she was standing there once more, this time holding a scratch sheet of her own in her hand. Before I'd had time to think twice, she'd passed it to me, and I'd taken it by reflex and was holding it. It's very difficult not to take something into your hand when it's extended to you unexpectedly and you're not on guard.

"I had this downstairs in my clothes locker," she said in a cracked whisper, her young-old eyes glittering with anticipation. "I ran down and got it."

To thrust it back at her and close the door on her, I didn't have the heart to do that. Admittedly, it's this type of softness that gets us into most of our difficulties, and I sometimes think I was born with more than my fair share.

She stood there waiting eagerly, and I was expected to say something.

"Come in a minute," I said, very businesslike, to gain time.

She followed me in, but left the door narrowly ajar, I suppose so that she could claim, technically, to be just completing the room in case one of her superiors should happen along.

I went over by the window and scanned it thoughtfully. The thoughtfulness was just a defense pose. I was actually scanning it in blank consternation, wondering what on earth to do with it now that I had it. It was just a list of horses' names, most of them freakish names at that. No schoolboy caught unprepared when called on to stand up in class and recite some preassigned lesson, or found out cheating on an examination paper, ever felt more miserably guilty than I did or wished more that he could drop through the floor and vanish safely from sight.

The momentary glow the unsought impersonation had given me was quite gone, and all I felt now was a skittish unease. But by this time it was a sheer impossibility for me to undeceive her. I didn't have the moral courage to do it any more. Not after she'd taken the trouble to go all the way down to the basement and back, and stolen risky time off between rooms to come to me with it. It should have been done in the first place or not at all. And her inevitable answer, "why didn't you say so in the first place?" would have put me in too fatuous, ridiculous a light, even in my own eyes, to be endured.

It was no good saying there wasn't a pencil. The room was full of them, and even if it hadn't been, I had a feeling she was resourceful enough to immediately produce one of her own, just as she had the scratch sheet. In any case, one wasn't indispensable. I could have given her the selection by word of mouth just as well, we both knew that.

To quiet my own conscience, which was rightfully uneasy at what I was about to do, I asked her just one question before proceeding.

"You're going to bet anyway, whether I give you a tip or not, is that right?" I said to her.

"Oh, yes, I always do," she agreed. "Only, I never win. This time it'll be different."

That eased my scruples considerably. She would lose her money either way I told myself, whether I was involved or not, so I needn't feel guilty about being the cause of it.

I went over to a table, spread the scratch sheet out flat on it, and bent over it, palms akimbo. She came over and stood close, all attention. I unclipped a mechanical pencil from my inside coat pocket and thumbed down the plunger on it in readiness.

The names were listed there perpendicularly but it was useless to pick one rationally. They were all alike to me. Probably, at that, she knew as much or more about it than I did.

I knew she would be looking down at the sheet, as I was, and not at my face, so I closed my eyes briefly, speared the pencil down, and twirled a quick, partly open oblong on the paper. When I opened them and looked, it encompassed the first syllable of one of the names, only. The rest of the letters had escaped outside it. However, the first three were definitely, unmistakably enclosed by it. They were "Neo-," although I can no longer remember what the rest of it was. But it was either "Neophyte" or "Neon-light," one of those two (and if it was the former, how appropriate it was, I have often thought since!). It was the fifth entry in a start of six, and as I looked further I noticed it had very poor odds down against it.

"There," I said with assumed nonchalance, as though I was in the habit of doing this every day. "That what you want?" And I restored the pencil to the inside of my pocket.

Her thanks were effusive. They were so fervent they were almost embarrassing. One would have thought I had given her Aladdin's lamp, with which to open up all the riches of the world. As she backed and talked out of the room she kept staring at the name on the paper, as though to make sure it wouldn't rise up and fly away, and then at me, and then at the paper once more. She was holding it extended between her two hands as though it were some sacred scroll or holy writ.

"Don't bet too much, now," was the last thing I said to her. "Remember, nothing's ever a sure thing."

"I can't, on what I make," she retorted in her cracked voice. "Not if I expect to eat!"

The door closed.

I never saw her again from that day on; never again laid eyes on her.

But not too long after, as I was keying my door to go into the room one day, a very amiable-looking, heavily built colored woman suddenly thrust her head out of the room next door, which she had been engaged in making up, and asked me solicitously: "Want me to make your room up for you now?"

"Anytime you say," I answered indifferently. "I'm in no hurry."

But she promptly deserted the one she had been occupied with—which obviously hadn't been completed yet—and came in then and there, leaving the other one half made up and with the door standing wide open.

Such attentiveness struck me as a little unusual, particularly as I hasn't asked for this priority, but I was too unsuspecting to immediately detect any motive in it. Meanwhile, with a great billowing up and deflating setting down again of sheets, as though a windblown regatta race were crossing and recrossing my bed, she set to work.

Her diligence was unparalleled. I had never known that a hotel maid could be that conscientious before.

She kept insisting over and over, "Now if there's anything you want, anything a little special or extra, you just let me know. I'm _____ ," and she gave me her first name, which I have since forgotten. "You just call the housekeeping department and ask for me, and I be at your door before you can say Jackie Robinson."[3]

And this went on and on.

"You sure you got enough blankets in here? You wouldn't want me to bring another?"

"The weather's been very warm," I pointed out. "I've always liked to sleep light."

"Could you use an extra pillow?"

"I'm fine this way. I don't like my head propped up too high."

"How about ashtrays? I notice you smoke heavy. I could put one over there by the window for you."

"There are three in the room already," I demurred. "And it might be better for me if I smoked a little less."

I thought to myself, this hotel maid is a paragon. She's almost too good to be true.

"Are you going to be the maid on this floor from now on?" I asked her, anticipating limitless bounties.

"Yes," she beamed. "I got this floor now. They transferred me up from the third. I axed them to, and I got seniority rights, I been here the longest."

Some sort of behind-the-scenes union politics or wire pulling had been in back of this, I supposed vaguely. But why did she have a preference for this particular floor? Weren't they all about the same, I wondered; the same number of rooms and all that?

"Well, what happened to that old lady who was in here the other day?" I asked her. "She wasn't dismissed, was she?" And I thought, troubled, perhaps at last they realized that she was getting too old, and I felt a momentary pang of regret. She'd been such a blithe, chipper little soul.

"Missis Clark?" she repeated. "Oh, no sir, she's here yet. She got my old floor. She's doing fine. You know that horse you pick' for her the other day? It came in."

"What?" I shrilled. If I hadn't checked my voice in time it would have come out an upper-register squeal, but I managed to hold it down at least to high tenor. I was so taken back I even braced a leg behind me, the way you do when you think you're about to stagger.

"You're joking," I finally managed to mouth, slack-jawed. "No sir, I' not joking. It came in. I thought you knew that." And she looked at me a little blankly, as though failing to understand how someone "on the inside," such as I was supposed to be, wouldn't know such a thing. But the thought didn't remain with her long enough to trouble her, I could see that.

"She came back twice to your door to thank you, but I guess you were out," she added.

I still couldn't get past the original stunning impact. "She bet on it?" I marveled. "And it came in?"

Anyone less absorbed in her own purposes and intentions would have noticed there was something off-key in the way I was taking the whole thing, but she didn't seem to.

"Course she bet on it. You picked it for her, didn't you?"

"You haven't any idea how much she won, have you?"

I would give a lot, as a writer whose every instinct is to bring a story around full circle, shape it, and give it a sudden sharp twist at the end, to be able to say here that she made a large winning, a killing, as they call it, and was able to give up her job and spend her few remaining years in leisure and comfort, even if not affluence. But life doesn't produce rounded-out stories, only formless little sketches that are always left open at both ends. Even life as a whole is that: one long formless sketch, left open at both ends. One end birth, the other death. This little anecdote, therefore, must stick to the truth, or else there is no point in relating it at all.

"Either forty, or forty-four dollars, something like that," she said. "She told us, but I can't remember which it was."

It had had very high odds quoted against it, that much I was able to recall myself. She might, at that rate, have placed no more than a two-dollar bet.

"But it's still better than working all week," she added, and quite logically too, I thought. "She got it for doing nothing."

And then finally it came. I'd known it was coming sooner or later, ever since the conversation had gotten around to "Missis Clark" and her successful wager. For that had given this new maid the opening she'd been angling for from the moment she'd first come into the room. It explained her almost fanatic devotion to my needs and comfort, and it also explained her preemption of this particular floor away from the aforesaid "Missis Clark." It explained a lot of things that I hadn't had the wit to realize in time.

"I don't suppose you' got a little tip like that you could let *me* have? I could sua use one."

And picking up my hairbrush, which stood on its back on the dressing chest, she scrupulously scoured the very small place it had occupied with her dustcloth, then restored it exactly to where it had been before. I couldn't make out whether this was to keep the hairbrush clean from the dresser, or keep the dresser clean from the hairbrush. Most likely, though, it was to keep her hands busy while she was waiting for my momentous answer.

I saw plainly that I'd gotten myself into one devil of a predicament. If I did give her a tip it would be worthless and she'd lose her money. If I refused to give her one she'd be offended and resentful, and rightfully so, and point out that I'd given one to "Missis Clark," so why not to her? Either way, I simply couldn't win.

The only solution I could see was to not give her one, and yet not refuse to at the same time. In other words, put her off, procrastinate, gain all the time I could.

"Will you let me think about it?" I said, oracular. "I have to give it a little thought. I can't tell you anything right now."

"Oh, that's all right, that's all right," she hastened to assure me, and I could see she was overjoyed at having won even a half promise like that. "I can wait. Just 'long as you don't forget me."

The horses weren't running that particular day anyway, but that was neither here nor there, as they most certainly were running on the upcoming weekend and that was only about three days off.

I knew it was a cowardly, better say unfair, thing to do, let her build her hopes over a period of several days and then have them brought down. But isn't that what hopes are made for, to be brought down? If they succeed, then they aren't hopes any more. There are always new hopes to come after them, anyway. Whereas money lost by a hard-working person isn't that easily replaced.

I suppose, some might say, hard-working people with little money shouldn't bet on horses! On the contrary, I think they're the very ones who should, rather than the rich. Even if they lose, and they usually do, it brings an excitement, a pleasure into their drab lives that is sorely lacking. Moreover, they can't lose to the point of ruination, they haven't that much money to bet in the first place. Whereas with the rich it's just a fashionable pose. If they lose, it means nothing. If they win, it means less.

"I'll think about it," I repeated. "Just give me a little time."

"See, I don't want this just for myself alone," she went on to explain, as though feeling that this selflessness on her part might help to win me over. "I believe in sharing a good thing with those who works alongside of me. So we' getting up a so't of a pool, in a way, and whichever horse you gives us for Sa'day's race—"

"Who?" I gasped in consternation. "Who is?"

"All of us floor maids, one on each floor, is chipping in, and the bus boy in the coffee shop, he's that little Filipino fellow, is putting up something, and we' trying to get the two girls on the elevator to come in with us too. See, the more we has to put down, the more we stands to make."

Arithmetically, I didn't think she was right. The odds were fixed, so you got back only the set ratio that they were fixed at, whether two to one or a hundred to one. True, the larger your bet, the more you got back. But then the larger your bet, the more of what you got back was originally your own money, so you were actually getting back less, pro rata. That was the way I saw it, in my inexperience.

But that wasn't what chiefly concerned me. It was the way the thing had snowballed up as it went rolling along, almost overnight you might say, that appalled me the most. There seemed to be no way of stopping it anymore. The story must have been all over the hotel by this time, at least among the working staff. I might have been adroit enough to ward off one maid, or maybe even two of them, but I couldn't go on indefinitely warding off half the employees in the building.

The last thing she said, having finally completed her duties (and I don't think any hotel room ever received the attention mine did that day), was "What time you want me to do your room tomorrow? I' come and get you anytime you say."

"Not too early," I said. "When you see the tag come off." And I promised myself, early or late, you won't find me in it when you do come, if I can help it.

"What happens if it rains?" I suggested, looking up at her hopefully.

"Well, if the track get' too muddy, of course, they put it off till it dry out. But it ain't gonna." And she pointed irrefutably to the little tabletop radio. "Didn't you hear what they say this mo'ning? Five straight days of sunshine coming up. Not a single cloud anywhere along the whole Northwes' Pacific Coas'."

Even in that I had no luck, I reflected. Although seriously even I, in my abysmal ignorance, knew that a rained-out race was simply run off the following night.

"I'll see you," she said gaily. "Take care of yourself."

I knew how she meant it, and I smiled wryly and uncomplimented. I was of considerable pecuniary value, and therefore not now expendable. "I always have, until now," I answered drily.

But she made her meaning even more clear than it had been (although actually only in jest, of course). "Make sua you do at leas' till after Sa'day," she chortled. "We' counting on you."

"I'll try," I said, and after she'd gone out I went over and threw the double lock on the door, to make sure she wouldn't find some excuse for coming back again.

This time I didn't just shrug and chuckle. I sank into a chair and held my head between both hands.

It was an irremediable situation. Not too tragic, not too ponderous, it's true, but with just enough prickly discomfort attached to make it uninviting. And I've never cared much for discomfort when it's not basic, inevitable, implicit in a given condition; in other words when there's a choice offered. But then who does?

If I admitted the hoax, I was the laughingstock of the hotel. And even laughter that is good-natured and not malicious is better when directed elsewhere and not at yourself. If I let it continue and risked giving another tip, the bubble would instantaneously burst (for I knew that never again for all the rest of my life would I probably be able to pick a winning horse; such a fluke occurs only once, and usually the very first time), and I would cost some hard-working person or persons their hard-earned money, and justifiably become an object of resentment and ill will, with all the deteriorations in service and courtesy that such an attitude can entail despite the best efforts of the higher echelons. There is even a way of saying "Good Morning" or "Yes, Sir" that is intrinsically a snub and a sneer in itself. And if I refused to give any further tips, I would be considered selfish, stingy, disobliging, and arouse pretty much the same disfavor as in the other case.

And everyone likes to be liked. I know at least that I do. Perhaps I haven't enough liking for myself, perhaps that is why I seem to want so much to have the liking of others.

Another thing: it seemed to me, wise now after the event, that there had been, only just within the last few days, a subtle, indefinable change toward me on the part of even those who were not manual workers, the upper brackets, so to speak. Before now they had been correctly courteous and courteously correct, as in all hotels, but no more than that. Now a little extra something had been added that wasn't there before. If not a little extra attention, then a little extra interest. It was so intangible you couldn't put a finger on it, and yet to my mind at least it was unmistakable.

For instance, the hostess in the Coffee Shop, whose duties definitely did not include clearing used dishes off tables so that new arrivals could sit down, elected to do so for me in the little booth I picked to sit in. Nor was the waitress otherwise occupied, for she stood by with idle hands watching her do so.

Then, the assistant manager, Mr. MacDonald, didn't simply look up from his duties as I happened to pass the desk, give me a polite but perfunctory "Good Morning," and then immediately look down again, as he had been doing all along until now. He continued gazing curiously after me long after I had gone by. I knew this to be so, because I happened to turn my head, from some distance away, and I found him to be still looking after me. His head was even extended slightly out past the edge of the desk to obtain a better view.

And even the man who played the piano in the cocktail bar each night, a place in which I had barely shown my face (I don't like those dimly lit grottoes, in me they bring about a certain melancholy), and with whom I had up until then exchanged not a solitary word, crossed the entire width of the lobby one night to offer me a special make of cigarette he used, wrapped in a brown Russian leaf, in place of the one he saw me about to take up and light. Nor was this just an attempt at good public relations on his part, to win me as a customer, for in the brief chat that followed he admitted that he didn't like those places himself, didn't blame me for avoiding them, and only spent his own time in them because he had to make a living.

There were many other instances such as these, which I can no longer remember, all of them equally trifling it is true, but all of them pointing pretty much the same way: as if I had become the golden egg of the hotel. Or at least a feathered (I suppose I should say crewcutted) bird capable at any time of laying one.

This, then, was the situation as it had now developed. Admittedly minor key, but unwelcome nevertheless. About like a pin sticking into your shirt or a piece of gravel inside your shoe or an eyelash sticking into your eye. I was on the point of being hounded by the lower ranks of the hotel staff, and if I hadn't yet been solicited by the upper ranks, it was only their greater reticence that was holding them back. I felt sure that would come too.

I won't say that it worried me. That would be an exaggeration in the opposite direction. But I did review it in my mind after I'd come in that night and sat there by the window looking out at the vivaciously beautiful nightlights of Seattle and wondering vaguely in which direction Longacres lay, and if it could be seen from where I was. Probably not, for it was way out toward Renton and must have been dark all night, since there was no racing on that night. And as I thought it over I couldn't help grinning sheepishly in my mind (if there is such a thing as grinning in one's own mind). But I knew there was really only one thing to do to tactfully put an end to it.

In the morning I packed my bag, called down for a bellman, and gave up my room. It wouldn't be accurate to say that this horse-tipster affair played a main part in my leaving; other, more important considerations actuated that. But it did advance it by a day or two if nothing else. Beautiful weather was at hand, and I think I would have stayed on over the weekend at least, if it hadn't been for that damnable Saturday race coming up.

As we stepped out into the hall, he in the lead, she was at work in a room on the opposite side of the hall from mine. That could easily be seen by the door standing open at full width. I won't say that I tiptoed past (for I owe it as much to be truthful where I myself am concerned as to the other participants in this minute narration) but my state of mind was that of a tiptoer as I did go past. I looked in as I went by. But coincidence or timing or whatever you want to call it, was very kind to me. For she was definitely in there, her paraphernalia was to be seen all over the room, but at the moment that I passed by, she must have been inside the tiled bath enclosure, so that we were cut off from direct sight of one another.

As if that had not been bad enough, the door of this particular room lay straight smack across from the elevator shaft doors, so that we had to stand there waiting with our backs to her the moment or two that it took the car to come up for us. But I maneuvered deftly (and cravenly) around to the other side of him, out of direct range, and moved closer in against the wall. And thus she never saw me from first to last.

It wasn't that she would have said anything, what could she have said? It was that hurt, wordless look that I quailed from. Her hopes of a winning, all gone.

Even in him, the bellman, I thought I detected a slight constraint, an overtone of reproof, when he handed my bag into the back of the car, thanked me and said "Goodbye, sir." Or was it imaginary?

And I admit I stole a guilty look back through the rear window as my cab pulled away.[4] But the entrance stood empty. No irate bellman or maid or porter or anyone else had come out to shake a thwarted accusing fist after me.

Notes

Epigraph

The epigraph to *Blues of a Lifetime*, from Thomas Mann's 1901 novel *Buddenbrooks*, conveys the decision of an aging patriarch to reflect upon his life. The full passage reads:

Thomas Buddenbrook had played now and then throughout his life with an inclination to Catholicism. But he was at bottom, none the less, the born Protestant: full of the true Protestant's passionate, relentless sense of personal responsibility. No, in the ultimate things there was, there could be, no help from outside, no mediation, no absolution, no soothing-syrup, no panacea. Each one of us, alone, unaided, of his own powers, must unravel the riddle before it was too late, must wring for himself a pious readiness before the hour of death, or else part in despair. [From H.T. Lowe-Porter, trans. (1924), rpt. New York: Knopf, 1955: 523.]

I

[1]The typewriter for which this chapter is named was mentioned in the dedication of Woolrich's first "black" (*noir*) novel, *The Bride Wore Black* (1940). It was Woolrich's first typewriter. However, the text of *Blues* was typed on another, later typewriter, which "looked different" from the old Remington Portable.

[2]Because the chronology of *Blues of a Lifetime* is problematic, readers should view this claim with some skepticism.

[3]Woolrich's first love is the subject of "The Poor Girl." His third love culminated in a brief, unconsummated marriage to actress Gloria Blackton (see Nevins' *Cornell Woolrich* and appendix). Nothing is known of his second love.

[4]This passage—on personality, pretense, and truth—casts doubt on Woolrich's motives in writing *Blues of a Lifetime*. After having admitted episodes of "lying to myself" and mistreating his friends, why does Woolrich claim the virtue "self-honesty"? Furthermore, we know Woolrich *did* in fact lie about his birth year to Stanley J. Kunitz (editor, First Supplement, *Twentieth Century Authors*), saying he was born in 1906 instead of his actual birth year, 1903. And this particular lie has been repeated, beginning as early as 1927, when Woolrich ended an unhappy college experience at Columbia University (see the next note). Francis M. Nevins, Jr., author of *Cornell Woolrich: First You Dream, Then You Die*, (New York: Mysterious P, 1988) has compiled a variety of Woolrich's (self-) deceptions.

[5]Woolrich attended Columbia University during 1921-1926, but after his five years' study he failed to graduate. According to his transcript, several extended absences in the spring 1925 semester led to failing grades, even in English (his best subject), and to academic probation. One of his Columbia classmates, historian Jacques Barzun, recalls Woolrich's sudden disappearance (interview in 1985 television documentary by Christian Bauer, *Nacht*

ohne Morgen: Die dunkle Welt des Cornell Woolrich). This evidence indicates that Woolrich may have contracted jaundice in March 1925. (This story takes place during 1922-1923.)

On the other hand, Woolrich has given alternative accounts of his illness and his college experience. In 1944, for example, he told A.L. Furman, editor of *Third Mystery Companion* (New York: Gold Label, 1945), that he became a less "conscientious" student after publishing *Cover Charge* (1926). He had explained, in 1927, "I made $12,000 in my first full year of writing, but flunked in German (I think it was). I never did make up the extra credits I needed for that. It was more fun writing. And a lot more remunerative" (*College Humor* January 1927: 395). Still another version of his illness is related by Ellery Queen in the introduction to *The Ten Faces of Cornell Woolrich* (New York: Simon, 1965): "A common, everyday occurrence (how prophetic!) led Cornell Woolrich into a writing career...an old soft-soled gym shoe...rubbed one of his heels raw, an infection developed, and Woolrich had to keep his foot up on a chair for weeks" (9).

[6] Woolrich's maternal grandfather, George A. Tarler, lived at 239 West 113th Street in Morningside Heights, a few blocks east of Columbia University across Morningside Park. At the time, Spanish Harlem lay farther east, beyond Lenox Avenue. (See the maps in the 1939 *WPA Guide to New York City*, rpt. New York: Pantheon, 1982: 255, 293.)

[7] Woolrich's father, Genaro Hopley-Woolrich, is a shadowy figure about whom little is known. (The fullest account is provided in Nevins' *Cornell Woolrich*.) He seems to have been working as an American mining engineer in Mexico during the 1910-1920 Mexican Revolution. According to *McClure's* Magazine, August 1927, Woolrich traveled with his father in Mexico and the Caribbean as a youth, then returned to New York to live with his mother in 1918. Sometime earlier, his parents had become estranged. No one knows the circumstances of the Woolrich family during those early years.

[8] When George A. Tarler and his wife Sarah ("Sadie") Cornell Tarler moved into the house of West 113th Street, their household included two teenaged daughters, Claire Attalie Tarler (Woolrich's mother) and her sister Estelle. An older son, George Cornell Tarler, had already established his independence when the Tarlers moved to Morningside Heights.

[9] According to a wedding announcement for George Cornell Tarler, Woolrich's grandfather George A. Tarler was, during the 1870s, "one of the pioneers in the Mexican and Central American export and import trade" (*New York Times* 20 February 1927: Sect. 2, pg. 6).

[10] (Franz) Xaver Scharwenka (1850-1924), a Polish-German pianist, composer, and teacher, ran his own conservatory of music in New York during 1891-1898, after which he returned to Berlin. He was renowned for his sonorous interpretations of Chopin and for the "melodic charm and graceful dance-like rhythms" of his own compositions [*The New Grove Dictionary of Music and Musicians* (London: Macmillan, 1980), Vol. 16].

[11] Woolrich's typescript reads "they are rather than studious."

[12] James W. Gerard (1867-1951), U.S. Ambassador to the German Imperial Court, wrote a memoir of his diplomatic work, *My Four Years in Germany* (New York: Doran, 1917), in which he informed Americans of "the gravity of the situation; because...the military and naval power of the German Empire is unbroken" (vii).

[13] Woolrich's impression of the popular fiction predating WWI is echoed by at least one contemporary historian. Alan Valentine writes that in 1913 popular "fiction was on its way from overromantic myth to overstark reality, from excessive self-adulation to excessive self-debunking" [*1913: America Between Two Worlds* (New York: Macmillan, 1962) 183].

[14] British novelist Robert Hichens (1864-1950) was author of *The Garden of Allah* (New York: Grosset, 1904), an exotic romance about a monk in love with a woman he meets in the desert. *Elizabeth and Her German Garden* (Chicago: Conkey, 1901) was

published anonymously by Countess Mary Annette Beauchamp Russell (1866-1941). One sequel, based on her miserable second marriage (to John Francis Stanley Russell), was titled *Vera* (Garden City, NY: Doubleday, 1921). Readers may wonder whether it is sheer coincidence that Woolrich's first love—the "poor girl"—and the female lead of his first novel, *Cover Charge* (1926), are also named "Vera."

[15]"Jazz Beau," which is the most innovative chapter in *Cover Charge*, begins with an utterly nondescript line: "Alan's career begins from the moment he bought a three-cent paper at a newsstand and opened it at the 'Help Wanted, Male' column, a thing he had never done before" (111). This chapter seems to have been the "nucleus" of that first novel. In a letter to *McClure's* Magazine, published August 1927, Woolrich claimed that his fiction salvaged an English course that he was failing under Dr. John Erskine: "Some fragmentary stuff written after midnight and turned in in desperation, struck his fancy, won me a high grade and became the nucleus from which *Cover Charge* developed" (32).

[16]Woolrich's composition methods remind one of Mozart, who once explained, "the committing to paper is done quickly enough, for every thing is, as I said before, already finished; and it rarely differs on paper from what it was in my imagination" [see Edward Holmes, *The Life of Mozart, Including His Correspondence* (London: Chapman, 1845) 318]. In 1954, Woolrich wrote to Stanley J. Kunitz that he typically wrote first drafts in longhand, making occasional revisions and changes as he typed the manuscript (First Supplement to *Twentieth Century Authors*). A writer who knew Woolrich during the 1960s, Steve Fisher, describes his work habits this way: "Sitting in that hotel room he wrote at night—continuing through until morning, or whenever the story was finally completed. He did not revise, polish, and I suspect did not even read the story over once it was committed to paper.   For that reason (he admitted to me) by the time he was near the end he was almost exhausted and often closed   [stories] off abruptly—with little or no hint as to the final fate of his characters" ["Cornell Woolrich: '—I Had Nobody,' " *The Armchair Detective* 3 (1968/1969) 164].

[17]Nevins believes Woolrich and his mother visited Europe in 1931. He argues that, while in Biarritz, Woolrich intended to write *I Love You, Paris*, a novel whose fate is described in "Even God Felt the Depression."

[18]*Gitanes* were a French brand of cigarette.

[19]One such strip has survived among the Cornell Woolrich papers, Rare Books and Special Collections, Butler Library, Columbia University.

[20]In "Jazz Beau," Alan Walker lives in a low-rent Manhattan apartment working as a "soda jerker," a job he quits soon after taking it. Attending an evening at the Palais de Danse ("Pally dee Dawnce"), he is struck with the idea of becoming a "dancehall hound." Much of the chapter is a whirlwind of dancing and exotic salon activity, culminating in a jazz-happy block party on the night of the Armistice, 11 November 1918, where Alan meets his first love, a young Irish girl named Veronica ("Vera") Daugherty.

[21]Woolrich's plotting inspired occasional complaints from reviewers. For example, Isaac Anderson claimed that the plot of *The Bride Wore Black* "does not make particularly good sense" (*New York Times Book Review* 8 December 1940: 38). Kay Irvin said of *The Black Curtain* that much of it "attempts no connection with probabilities" (*New York Times Book Review* 15 June 1941: 17). Yet most reviewers felt that Woolrich's strengths outshined his weaknesses. For example, John Sutherland commented, in a review of the little-admired *Strangler's Serenade*, that "this able craftsman" Woolrich "still rigs his plot with a few inconsistencies, but uses them, as always to ricochet suspense to an almost unbearable pitch" (*New York Times Book Review* 11 March 1950: 20).

²²No passage of precisely this description can be found in Woolrich's early fiction. He seems to have in mind a scene in *Manhattan Love Song* that devotes several tedious paragraphs to the short interval between Wade's arrival in the lobby of Bernice Pascal's hotel and his subsequent ring at her apartment door (1932; rpt. Boston: Gregg, 1980: 48-50).

²³In 1934, eight years after publishing his first novel, the frothy *Cover Charge*, Woolrich published his first three suspense stories. Along with the ten stories he published during 1935, they are reprinted in *Darkness at Dawn: Early Suspense Classics*, eds. Francis M. Nevins, Jr., and Martin H. Greenberg (Carbondale: Southern Illinois UP, 1985).

²⁴The structure of *Cover Charge* is itself syncopated, like the jazz that inspired it. There are three parts consisting of nine chapters altogether ("Matinée," "Soirée," and "Gigolo and Gigolette") and an often uncertain plotline. Especially in the first few chapters one can find much fault with the novel: (1) crucial plot details are obscured in a wealth of minutiae; (2) the innovative jazz elements (in decor, costume, dance, and language) seem oddly external to the rest of the work; (3) the macaronic style seems a capricious blend of neo-Grecian, French, and jazz metaphors; and (4) since there is no organizing point of view, the characters undergo little or no psychological development. The book's experimental qualities, in sum, prove also to be its principal weakness. Therefore, the *New York Times* reviewer appears on one hand to praise it as being "a sort of subway, strap-hanging trip," while on the other hand complains that "Mr. Woolrich, by ignoring the principles of selection, blurs his tonal effects" ("In the Jazz Manner," rev. of *Cover Charge*, 21 March 1926: 8). Incidentally, it may have been this reviewer's preference for the chapter "Bacchanale" that inspired Woolrich to treat a similar subject at greater length in his next novel, *Children of the Ritz* (New York: Boni, 1927).

²⁵For brief biographies of Red Nichols and George Olsen, see Volume 3 of Roger D. Kinkle, *The Complete Encyclopedia of Popular Music and Jazz 1900-1950*, 4 vols. (New Rochelle, NY: Arlington, 1974). As a cornet player and band leader, Nichols recorded "Alexander's Ragtime Band," "Five Feet Two, Eyes of Blue," "Ballin' the Jack," "Dinah," "Tea for Two," "Peg o' My Heart," and "Poor Butterfly" (b/w "A Pretty Girl Is Like a Melody"). Band leader Olsen recorded many hits too, including "Everything I Have Is Yours" and "Zip-a-Dee-Doo-Dah." His recording of "Ida, Sweet as Apple Cider" sold more than a million copies in 1927. It was Olsen's band who introduced a new song at the Hotel Pennsylvania on 24 October 1929, a day now remembered as Black Thursday, for the great stock market crash. The song was "Happy Days Are Here Again."

²⁶Born on 4 December 1903, Woolrich turned sixteen as the 1920s were about to begin.

²⁷The "episode with Vera" is narrated in "The Poor Girl."

²⁸According to Marian Trimble, Gloria Blackton's sister, Woolrich had suppressed one key aspect of his personality—an inclination toward homosexuality. In an interview with Francis M. Nevins, Jr., quoted in *Cornell Woolrich*, Trimble claims that Woolrich entertained sailors while on his honeymoon, keeping a detailed diary of his exploits and of his low opinion of Gloria and her family. The diary, she alleges, was destroyed by Woolrich, whose fiction is occasionally homophobic.

²⁹Because Woolrich was both diabetic and alcoholic (drinking heavily after his mother's death), a minor leg infection became gangrenous, resulting in the partial amputation of his right leg in April 1968. His death that September may have been hastened by drinking. For a vivid depiction of Woolrich's last days, see Barry N. Malzberg's "Woolrich" [rpt. *The Fantastic Stories of Cornell Woolrich*, eds. Charles G. Waugh and Martin H. Greenberg (Carbondale: Southern Illinois UP, 1981) 329-334].

[30]The phrase "Valley of Anahuac" denotes the valley also known as the Valley of Mexico, which marks the general location of Mexico City. The valley, featuring many canals and lagoons as well as Lakes Texcoco and Zumpango, is bounded on the east by Sierra Nevada (noted for two majestic snow-capped volcanoes, Popocatépetl and Iztaccíhuatl) and on the south by a volcanic range that separates the Southern Highlands from the Southern Sierra Madre. According to Ronald Atkin, author of *Revolution! 1910-20* (New York: Day, 1970), "Iztaccíhuatl" means "Woman in White" (10), not "Our Lady of the Snows," the name given it by Blair Giraldy, the young hero of Woolrich's fourth novel, *A Young Man's Heart* (73, 104). A contemporary map of Mexico can be found in the July 1916 issue of *National Geographic*.

[31]Woolrich seems to be purposefully vague about Ken, Mrs. Collins, Ken's young female friends, and neighbors Carolyn and Helen (described later in Chapter 1), as well as about people described in later chapters of *Blues of a Lifetime*.

[32]Historian Jacques Barzun (see note 5) also recalls the veteran-students at Columbia during the mid-1920s: "These elders were not only mature chronologically, they were tempered by the experience of evil. Some were bitter, others cynical and gay, many were highly gifted; they led everything in the College without even trying... [Partly through] the intermittent friendships that bridged the unusual gap between senior and sophomore, at every turn that special influence made for ripening" ["As We Were," *University on the Heights*, ed. Wesley First (Garden City, NY: Doubleday, 1969) 89-93; quoting from 91].

[33]"I'm Just Wild About Harry" was the big hit of a 1921 all-black musical called *Shuffle Along* (Eubie Blake, composer; Nobel Sissle, lyricist). In these early days of the "single" record, few had a "B" side at all. Woolrich probably heard a recording by Lanin's Southern Serenaders (Acme 2024; rec. July 1922, New York). By 1925 the song was available in two other instrumental versions too. The first vocal rendition would not be recorded, however, until 1930, by Red Nichols and His Five Pennies, with Jack Teagarden singing the melody (Brunswick 6833; rec. 3 February 1930, New York). [See Brian Rust, *Jazz Records 1897-1942*, 4th rev. ed. (New Rochelle, NY: Arlington, 1978) I: 141, 935, II: 1142, 1173.]

[34]It was during 1931-1957, while Woolrich lived with his mother, that he published all his important suspense novels, including his entire "black" (*noir*) series.

[35]Woolrich's typescript reads, at this point, "Every meant an eviction."

[36]Since Ken is supposedly a senior at the time of this conversation, he could not in reality be planning to type a master's thesis a few months later.

[37]Woolrich's phrase "biological essays" is as oblique a reference to sexual activity as his earlier "high-spot" was to an erection.

[38]Having devoted his last few years to real estate, George A. Tarler died of heart disease on 25 April 1925 (see his obituary in the *New York Herald Tribune* 26 April 1925, Section 1, page 21).

[39]Claire Attalie Woolrich died on 6 October 1957, evidently of heart failure.

[40]Woolrich was an only child. Uncle George Cornell Tarler left behind only a stepson when he died in 1945 (see the obituary in the *New York Times* 28 December 1945: 15). Therefore, if Woolrich were the "only grandson" to George A. Tarler, his Aunt Estelle Tarler Garcia must have borne no sons before her father's death.

[41]Giacomo Puccini's opera *Madame Butterfly* depicts the tragic romance of American lieutenant Pinkerton and Japanese maiden Cio-Cio-San (whose name had been spelt "Cho-Cho-San" in the original David Belasco play). During most of 1912, having a December birthdate, Woolrich was eight years old. Perhaps he first saw the opera during that year.

⁴²Mexico City's Palacio de Bellas Artes (Palace of Art) is a marble building designed
by Adamo Boari in an Art Nouveau style. Commissioned under the presidency of Porfirio
Diaz, it was begun in 1900 but not completed until 1934. The stage features a glass mosaic
curtain weighing 22 tons and fashioned by Tiffany's Studios, New York, according to
a Gerardo Murillo design. The curtain portrays the landscape of the Valley of Mexico
(Anahuac), including the two famous volcanoes. For photographs of the opera house under
construction, its interior, and a partial view of the glass curtain, see Anita Brenner, *The
Wind That Swept Mexico: The History of the Mexican Revolution 1910-1942* (New York:
Harper, 1943), photos 52 and 53.

⁴³"Row Row Row" (James V. Monaco, composer; William Jerome, lyricist) was
introduced in the *Ziegfield Follies of 1912* according to Kinkle I: 58. "The Skeleton Rag"
(Percy Wenrich, composer; Edward Madden, lyricist) was published as sheet music in 1911
by Jerome H. Remick and Co. [see John Edward Hasse, ed., *Ragtime: Its History, Composers,
and Music* (New York: Schirmer, 1985) 315].

⁴⁴Woolrich's nationalism is also voiced in some of his fiction. For example, in *A
Young Man's Heart*, Eleanor hums "My Country 'Tis of Thee" when summoned to dinner
by Mexican insurgent General Palacios (221). In an earlier scene, Blair has nightmares
that his father is confusing him for a Chinese man, one of the nationalities toward whom
the elder Giraldy is hostile (79).

⁴⁵Here is intended a slang use of the term "ringer"—meaning a contestant who has
entered a competition dishonestly.

⁴⁶As hinted earlier in these notes, Woolrich's 1930 marriage to Gloria Blackton ended
in separation three months later and was annulled in 1933. He did not remarry.

⁴⁷*Shore Leave*, a light musical feature based on a Hubert Osborne play, opened in
September 1925 at the Mark Strand theater on Times Square, Broadway and 47th Street.
The *New York Times* reviewer had little to recommend, admiring only the fit of Donald
Barthelmess' sailor uniform and finding the many naval scenes merely "very interesting"
(14 September 1925: 16).

⁴⁸The last line of this paragraph was squeezed into the typescript as an interlineal
addition to the text. Woolrich is evidently poeticizing his memories.

⁴⁹The publisher of *Cover Charge* (1926), Boni and Liveright, had offices at 61 West
48th Street during 1923-1929, after which the company moved to 31 West 47th Street.
Woolrich's "key-sheet" for this chapter, among the Columbia University Woolrich
manuscripts, gives the employee's name as "Miss Kaufman." As a first publisher, this
was a fortuitous "choice," since contemporary Boni and Liveright titles included Sherwood
Anderson, *Dark Laughter* (1925), Anita Loos, *Gentlemen Prefer Blondes* (1925), Ernest
Hemingway, *In Our Time* (1925), and William Faulkner, *Soldier's Pay* (1926). [See Carmen
R. Russell, "Boni and Liveright," *American Literary Publishing Houses, 1900-1980: Trade
and Paperback*, ed. Peter Dzwonkoski, *Dictionary of Literary Biography* 46 (Detroit: Gale,
1986) 57-63.] Nevins, in *Cornell Woolrich*, notes that other accounts of this acquisition
have also been published (26).

⁵⁰The final clause in Woolrich's closing sentence was added to the carbon copy of
his typescript, on a different typewriter, but not to the original. Woolrich's key-sheet indicates
that he had once planned to describe more details of his emotional state and day-to-day
trivia at the time before revealing the novel's acceptance.

II

¹Several homoerotic but ambiguous references occur in the opening pages of "The
Poor Girl," coloring the friendship between Woolrich and his boxer friend Frank Van

Craig. No family of this surname can be found in contemporary Manhattan telephone directories, indicating that the name, if not the person, may be fictitious.

²Why Woolrich writes here that he "had no father" is a mystery. In "Remington Portable NC69411" he claims that his father sent money from Mexico for his tuition at Columbia, which Woolrich began attending in 1921. Could it be that, after Woolrich's first semester or two, he lost his father—to death, divorce, or disappearance? Or does this comment, like the anecdotes he is known for telling about his father, simply indicate his ambiguous feelings for him?

One of these anecdotes is recorded by editor Martha Foley, in *The Story of STORY Magazine*, ed. Jay Neugeborn (New York: Norton, 1980): "A thin, shabby, shaking, hungry-looking man, he asked me, almost imploringly, 'If I send you a story, will you please read it?' 'Of course,' I told him. 'That's why I'm an editor. To read manuscripts.' Reassured, he told me about himself.... I remember his telling me of how his father had left his mother, and of how, as a boy, he had spent years with her roaming around the country in search of his father. I have never forgotten his leaning forward to me and saying earnestly, 'A search for a father is a search for God' " (209-210).

³During the late 19th century New York City was crisscrossed with the cable-operated, elevated ("el") trains, electrified in 1902, which recur in Woolrich's fiction. Riding the el, one could catch glimpses of life in many social strata, as well as "scenes of great beauty: skyscrapers at dusk, glittering rivers, dwindling streets" (see *The WPA Guide to New York City* 404). When the first underground ("subway") trains became operational in 1904, the elevated trains began to see their demise. Finally considered unsightly and dangerous, the els were demolished during Woolrich's lifetime beginning in 1938, when the Sixth Avenue el structure was razed by the city of Manhattan (405).

⁴No listing for a Gaffney in this section of the city can be found in contemporary Manhattan telephone directories.

⁵This section of "The Poor Girl" has been condensed by the editor.

⁶Despite this comment, "The Poor Girl" is evidently set during 1922-1923, when Woolrich attended his second year at Columbia, not his first.

⁷Woolrich was not admitted into Columbia University's prestigious School of Journalism, no doubt because of his average-to-poor undergraduate record (see note 5 to the first section). In any case, the Columbia professional schools were closed to all freshmen and sophomores, who would be studying general science and humanities subjects during those first two years.

⁸According to the 1925 New York City Directory, the Morningside Theatre (a neighborhood theatre owned by the Trocadero Amusement Co.) was located at 2139 8th Avenue.

⁹Woolrich's lengthy description of a banana split, the quintessential American ice cream parlor dessert, shows that he led an isolated existence after World War II. The dish has remained perennially popular, even if associated in our modern memory with the 1940s and 1950s. Incidentally, since the next four paragraphs are typed on a separate leaf in the typescript, they may represent a late addition to the autobiography.

¹⁰Morningside Park is situated just as Woolrich describes it. The pathway along which he and Vera walk offers a fairly direct route from his grandfather's street on the east side of the pathway (113th Street) to the intersection of 116th Street and Morningside Drive on the west.

¹¹"Ka-lu-a" was introduced in the review *Good Morning, Dearie* (Jerome Kern, composer; Anne Caldwell, lyricist), which ran for 265 performances beginning 1 November 1921 (Kinkle I: 120). The song was first recorded by the California Ramblers in New York, on 14 December 1921 (Rust I: 218) and not recorded again until 1930.

¹²This socioeconomic analysis of the geography of Manhattan echoes the thoughts of a chauffeur in Woolrich's second novel, *Children of the Ritz* (1927): "It wasn't far from lower Fifth Avenue to upper Amsterdam, but they were worlds apart. He... [passed] from electricity in amber globes to electricity in uncoated globes, and from that to gaslight in cast-iron jets; from telephones in inlaid cases to telephones upon the wall, and from that to no telephones at all (except at the corner drug store); from fifteen-story apartment houses full of California Japanese domestics to six-story flats full of radios; from head waiters to dumbwaiters; from studiously bad manners and *Scheherazade* and iced *crèmes de menthe* with emerald-green cherries to no manners whatever and comic strips and washing machines and Tom Mix. In other words, from lower Fifth to upper Amsterdam" (23-24).

¹³*The WPA Guide to New York City* describes this stone memorial to Carl Schurz (1829-1906), newspaper editor and presidential advisor to both Lincoln and Hayes. It was built in 1912 (290).

¹⁴The Schurz memorial is located directly across from a Roman Catholic church that Woolrich mistakenly remembers, in the typescript of *Blues of a Lifetime*, as Notre Dame de "Lorette" instead of "Lourdes."

¹⁵Woolrich was 18 as he entered the fall of 1922, so his 19th birthday evidently came during his romance with Vera.

¹⁶Woolrich's first sexual experience is described in Chapter 1, which takes place mostly in 1925. Does his puzzling claim to have "not a trace of recollection" of her mean only that he cannot remember her appearance, her personality? Or is there another problem for the biographer in this passage?

¹⁷In the fall of 1922 Woolrich's grandfather, George A. Tarler, was still alive, not having suffered his fatal heart attack of April 1925. Why then does Woolrich call himself "the only male" of his household?

¹⁸The 1922 New York City Directory shows that a William M. Lambert, of 801 Riverside Drive, was employed at Anthony Eisler & Co., located at 221 Canal Street. According to the 1926-1927 New York telephone directory, the Lamberts later moved across Morningside (and Central) Park to 150 East 93rd Street.

¹⁹According to the 1926-1927 New York telephone directory H. C. F. Koch & Co. was a dry goods store located at 132 West 125th Street.

²⁰See note 11 above. "April Showers" (Louis Silvers, composer; Buddy DeSylva, lyricist) was featured in an Al Jolson musical, *Bombo*, which opened on Broadway 6 October 1921 for 219 performances (Kinkle I: 119).

²¹The Municipal Archives of the City of New York contain Magistrate's Court Docket books for the 5th District. These records provide supplementary information about a fur coat theft reported in the *New York Times* (29 January 1923: 7) and in the *New York Tribune* (29 January 1923: 4). Nineteen-year-old model Helen Ryan, of 826 Columbus Avenue, checked her Hudson Bay seal coat in the cloak room of Tangoland, a "dancing school" located at 171 East 86th Street, on the evening of 26 January 1923. Sometime that evening, the dancing instructor who had checked the coat, sixteen-year-old Catherine Bennett, of 222 East 95th Street, shoved three coats, including Miss Ryan's, through a window of the dance hall. Her accomplice, twenty-one-year-old chauffeur Bernard Hanley was waiting in the alley to speed away with the stolen coats to his apartment at 1599 Avenue "A." Upon Miss Ryan's complaint, police investigation led to the stolen coats and the arrest of the thieves. Initially pleading not guilty to the charge of grand larceny, the two defendants evidently worked out a plea bargain, pled guilty to a lesser charge (on 9 February 1923), and were given a mild sentence, which is not specified in the docket

book. Reform school seems a credible alternative for the girl's sentence, because she was
a minor at the time of the incident.

[22]"Dearest, You're the Nearest to my Heart" (Harry Akst, composer; Benny Davis,
lyricist) was introduced in an Eddie Cantor musical, *Kid Boots*, which opened on Broadway
31 December 1923 for 67 performances (Kinkle I: 138, 144-145). "Down, Down Among
the Sleepy Hills of Ten, Ten, Tennessee" is evidently a lyric from "Ten little Fingers
and Ten Little Toes," also known as "Down in Tennessee" (Ira Schuster and Ed G. Nelson,
composers; Harry Pease and Johnny White, lyricists). This song was introduced in 1921
[see Roger Lax and Frederick Smith, eds., *The Great Song Thesaurus*, 2nd ed. (New York:
Oxford UP, 1989) 386].

III

[1]"Brother, Can You Spare a Dime?" (Jay Gorney, composer; E.Y. Harburg, lyricist)
was introduced in the 1932 Broadway musical *Americana* (Hinkle I: 239) and recorded
by Leo Reisman that year as Victor 24156 (246). This title, along with the lyrics from
other Depression-era songs, indicates how widespread economic strife had grown within
the few years since the 1929 stock market crash. Woolrich's dilemma might not have been
as dire as he makes out, according to Nevins in *Cornell Woolrich*, since his mother's
family must have had considerable wealth.

[2]During the Prohibition years of 1920-1933, bootleg alcohol, also called "bathtub gin,"
was unlawful to manufacture, possess, distribute, or drink in the United States. Illegal
establishments, called "speakeasies," sprang up in many large cities, notably New York,
providing both alcohol and entertainment.

"Silver Threads Among the Gold" was first recorded by Red Nichols and His World-
Famous Pennies 18 June 1934 and released as Bluebird B-5583 (Rust II: 1146).

[3]For a detailed description of the "Hoovervilles," see Edward Robb Ellis, "Food Riots
and Hoovervilles," Chapter 11 of *A Nation in Torment: The Great American Depression,
1929-1939* (New York: Coward-McCann, 1970) 143-157.

[4]Woolrich had received income from only six stories and three poorly received novels
since the Crash. His "Women Are Funny" appeared in the October 1932 issue of *Illustrated
Love*, following the story "Orchids and Overalls" the previous March. Also in 1932 came
his sixth novel, *Manhattan Love Song*, which had no British nor paperback sales. (See
Nevins 87, 100-101, 125-127.)

[5]*My Life*, by Isadora Duncan (New York: Horace Liveright, 1927), was published
shortly before the dancer's accidental death by strangulation. While riding for the first
time in an Italian sports car, the Bugatti, her shawl was caught in a wheel spoke. The
driver could stop quickly enough to save her.

[6]Japanese Gardens was a movie theater at Broadway and 97th Street. In the typescript
of *Blues of a Lifetime*, Woolrich remembers the name as "the Japanese Garden."

[7]Nevins believes that Woolrich completed *Manhattan Love Song* in 1931, while on
a European tour with his mother, a trip evidently undertaken in response to Woolrich's
estrangement from Gloria Blackton (see *Cornell Woolrich* 86-88). The novel *I Love You,
Paris* may also have been initiated there.

[8]*Can Can*, a 1953 Cole Porter musical, featured a song called "I Love Paris" [see
David Ewen, ed., *American Popular Songs: From the Revolutionary War to the Present*
(New York: Random, 1966) 173].

[9]As indicated earlier in these notes, one of Woolrich's key-sheets has survived—that
for Chapter 1 of *Blues of a Lifetime*. It is among the papers in the Cornell Woolrich
Archives at Columbia University.

¹⁰The only such notice in the January-April 1933 *New York Times* book pages reads: "The publishing firm of Alfred H. King, Inc., reports 1932 as a successful year and that it is doubling its floor space at 432 Fourth Avenue. John J. Trounstine, formerly of Longmans, Green, has just joined the King staff as assistant editor" (*New York Times* 23 January 1933: 11). Woolrich did not publish a book with Longmans, so his comment about knowing "Irwin" in 1927-1928 is puzzling.

¹¹Nevins does not name the hotel where Woolrich lived at this time (see *Cornell Woolrich* 100-101). A later episode indicates that it may have been located near the 81st Street RKO Theatre (at 81st and Broadway). Sometime by the mid-1930s, the Tarler home was sold, and Woolrich moved with his mother into the Hotel Marseilles, at Broadway and 103rd Street (in 1990 a retirement apartment community). As early as 1927-1928, Woolrich's mother was no longer listed in the telephone directory at the 113th Street address. Yet, later in this chapter, Woolrich will claim that his mother and aunt were still living there in 1933.

Eight Charles Drews are listed in the 1933-1934 New York City Directory. One Charles S. Drew, of 1182 Broadway, is named as vice-president of a company headquartered in Catonsville, Maryland. The other Charles Drews worked in the occupations of broker, shirt manufacturer, carpenter, engineer, radio instructor, elevator operator, and delicatessen owner.

¹²Both husbands may have been lost through divorce or estrangement. No obituary for Emilio M. Garcia appears in the *New York Times Index* for this period. And Woolrich's father, as previously noted, has left a confusing trail.

¹³During the 1930s (and longer), some of the most popular American radio shows were hosted by Kate Smith, Eddie Cantor, George Burns and Gracie Allen, and many more well-loved stars of the stage and screen of yesteryear.

¹⁴French author François, Duc de la Rochefoucauld (1613-1680) compiled a book of aphorisms called *Reflections, or Sentences and Moral Maxims* (1665). However, Woolrich is recalling one of English author John Heywood's (1497-1580) *Proverbes*, published in 1546: "Better is halfe a lofe than no bread" (Part 1, Chapter 11).

¹⁵Woolrich's claim not to have entered a church until 1933 is puzzling evidence of his ambivalence toward religion. This subject is amply discussed by Nevins (see, for example, *Cornell Woolrich* 3, 6-7, 14, 16-17, 105-106, 116-117, 122, 311). Depending on the exact location of "Irwin's" publisher, the church Woolrich visited that day may have been either the Church of the Holy Cross, located on 42nd Street between Eighth and Ninth Avenues (across from McGraw-Hill and the Port Authority Building), or St. Malachy's Church, at 49th Street and Eighth Avenue, across from the Hotel Mayfair in the Theater District. Both churches are close to subway stops that connect to the line Woolrich would have taken in 1933 to arrive at Times Square from Morningside Heights (and vice versa).

¹⁶Evidently a typist hired to type this section mistook Woolrich's *n* for a *v* in the words *lonely* and *loneliness* throughout this passage. Many corrections in ink are found in the typescript. It is an ironic confusion that would have delighted Woolrich, to wonder whether a church nave is a *lovely* or a *lonely* place.

¹⁷Maurice Ravel's *Bolero* was used to accompany a dance number in Earl Carroll's 1931 *Vanities* [see Arnold Shaw, *The Jazz Age: Popular Music in the 1920s* (New York: Oxford UP, 1987) 243]. Therefore, Woolrich did *not* fall prey to the theft of an ingenious idea. In fact, he himself stole it from Carroll.

The 1934 film *Bolero*, starring George Raft, Carole Lombard, Ray Milland, and Sally Rand, also features a climactic scene in which two ill-fated lovers dance to Ravel's *Bolero*. For those who wish to compare Woolrich's plot summary of *I Love You, Paris* to the plot of *Bolero*, a summary can be found in Jay Robert Nash and Stanley Ralph Ross,

The Motion Picture Guide, 12 vols. (Chicago: Cinebooks, 1985) I: 256). The film plot bears little resemblance to the plot of Woolrich's book (in the editor's opinion).

IV

[1]The date 20 February 1957 fell on a Wednesday, not a Tuesday, as Woolrich's typescript reads. President Eisenhower gave an important speech that was reported in the 21 February issue of the *New York Times*, in which he apologized for being hoarse before beginning the speech proper. This apology is quoted from the *Times* almost verbatim, indicating that Woolrich used this text while completing "President Eisenhower's Speech." On that occasion Eisenhower felt the need to explain to Americans why "the United Nations has no choice but to exert pressure upon Israel" to withdraw its invading troops from Egypt (see *New York Times* 21 February 1957: 4).

[2]On 29 September 1938, England, France, Germany, and Italy signed the so-called "Munich Pact" in that city. It granted Adolf Hitler his demand for more "living space" by ceding to him the Sudetenland of Czechoslovakia. The next spring, on 15 March 1939, Hitler violated his pledge to the world leaders, invading Prague in order to take over the rest of Czechoslovakia. When he invaded Poland on 1 September 1939, England declared war on Germany, and World War II had officially begun.

[3]According to Nevins, the hotel where Woolrich lived with his mother until her death in October 1957 was the Hotel Marseilles, at 104th and Broadway. However, the *New York Times* reported only one hotel fire during that year—one at the Hotel Brierfield, located at 215 West 83rd Street, between Broadway and Amsterdam (20 November 1957: 42; and 21 November 1957: 35).

[4]This quotation from Eisenhower's speech is written in longhand in Woolrich's typescript, within a space punctuated by two hyphens, as if he had written the chapter and then later consulted the *Times* to select appropriate quotations to insert. The old issues of the *Times* would have been available in the 1960s at the New York Public Library. This procedure is also followed for later quotations from the Eisenhower speech. The quotation at hand comes from the 39th paragraph.

[5]This quotation is from the 35th paragraph of Eisenhower's speech. See also note 4 above.

[6]These quotations are from the 21st and 28th paragraphs of Eisenhower's speech, respectively. See also note 4 above.

[7]A bizarre series of fires was set by a 12-year-old girl during the night of 19 November 1957 at the Hotel Brierfield. The story made good material for the "pulps" too, and was reported in the *New York Post* (20 November 1957: 3; and 21 November 1957: 3), the *New York Daily News* (20 November 1957: 4; and 21 November 1957: 4), and the *New York World-Telegram* (20 November 1957: 1), in addition to the *New York Times* (20 November 1957: 42; and 21 November 1957: 35). See also note 3 above.

The youngster, whose mother was a chorus dancer at the Flamingo in Las Vegas and who had been a showgirl in New York's Latin Quarter for eight years, was living with her grandparents at the hotel. The father and mother had been divorced.

Most of the fires were easily put out, some having been started in trash containers, overstuffed armchairs, or piles of rubbish in the hotel basement. Until the origin of the 11 fires was known, hotel workers, firemen and police were kept busy and frustrated. When questioned, the "Littlest Firebug" admitted that she got the idea from TV and that she "like the excitement they cause." A judge in the Children's Court ordered her taken to Bellevue Hospital for psychiatric examination.

If this incident were the basis for Woolrich's story of the fire, its details certainly seem quirky enough. Yet the Brierfield fires took place in November, almost exactly a month after Claire Attalie Woolrich's death, and apparently in a different hotel altogether from the one she had shared with her son. The connection with Eisenhower's speech is nil, including the timing, which may account for Woolrich's deliberate erasure of the subject of the radio address.

[8]At this point, Woolrich failed to insert a quotation from Eisenhower's speech, as he had intended, so the editor has selected a sentence from its 51st paragraph.

[9]This comment is reminiscent of a passage in Woolrich's novel *Night Has a Thousand Eyes*: "It began in such a little way. A drop. Yes, that was it, a drop.... There is no littler way in which a thing can begin than that.... Death has begun. Darkness has begun, there in the full jonquil-blaze of the dinner-table candles. Darkness. A spot no bigger at first than that spilled drop of consomme" (Chapter 2, opening paragraphs).

[10]Where Woolrich has used the term *engineer* in his typescript, the editor has substituted the term *mechanic*.

[11]Woolrich was always thin. See the various photographs, taken during the 1920s through the 1960s, that are reprinted in *Cornell Woolrich* (between pages 206 and 207).

[12]This lesion is evidently the one that developed into a gangrenous infection, eventually causing Woolrich's death. See *Cornell Woolrich* for more details, as well as note 29 to the first section.

V

[1]The Roosevelt Hotel, now known as the WestCoast Roosevelt Hotel, is located at 1531 7th Street in Seattle.

[2]The Longacres Race Track, site of thoroughbred horse racing, is located near I-405 and West Valley Highway, in Renton, approximately 15 miles from downtown Seattle.

[3]Jackie Robinson (1919-1972) was the first black player in baseball's major leagues, known for his first-rate batting average and his ability to steal bases. He signed with the Brooklyn Dodgers in 1947, had 10 impressive seasons, and was elected to the Baseball Hall of Fame in 1962.

[4]"Rear Window" is, of course, one of Woolrich's best-known titles, partly because of the Alfred Hitchcock film, adapted from the 1942 short story in 1954. The story was first published under the title "It Had to Be Murder" in *Dime Detective*, February 1942, and has had numerous reprints.

Appendix:
Fragments from the Woolrich Archives

Blues of a Lifetime was intended, at some point, to include a *sixth* section, in addition to the five that Woolrich completed. Among his papers is a table of contents showing "The Maid Who Played the Races" as the sixth chapter; however, no title is offered for the missing fifth chapter. Eventually Woolrich abandoned the idea of writing yet another "personal story." The table of contents recorded in his notebook, a 1937 Marquette-brand diary (in the archives at Columbia University), shows clearly that "The Maid Who Played the Races" should be the fifth and final chapter of his autobiography.

However, there is one glaring omission in this volume—the story of Woolrich's failed marriage. Nevins provides the fullest account available in his *Cornell Woolrich* (70-77). And a lengthy contemporary account can be read in the 9 July 1933 issue of the *Cleveland Plain Dealer*.

The following narrative (Part 1 of the Appendix) is made entirely of bits of prose (fiction) that can be found in the Woolrich archives at Columbia University. Read together, in this artificially edited sequence, they appear to tell the story of a failed marriage. Only the reader can judge how closely the fiction represents truth.

Part 2 is Woolrich's intended "ending" for his autobiography.

Part 1
Outline of a Missing Chapter?
...We had a little house-warming, just for and by and with, the two of us. No noisy noise, no noisy guests, nobody else. Just the two, we two, the me of it and the you. I brought in a bottle of Moet and Chandon, but we only had about one drink apiece of that (and in her case just a lip-wetting) and then, somehow, I don't know how, we started to talk.

"You're not afraid of me, are you?" I said at one point. I indicated the four sides of the room by swinging my upped thumb around them in a twirl. "Of this, and me, and tonight?"

"No," she said quite simply, looking straight at me, untroubled, unevasive. "You're my destiny. I've been coming straight toward you ever since I was born. You and this room, and this night...."

But mostly we went dancing.

After awhile we started to stay home about once a week.

Then after awhile we stayed home every second night or so.

Then after another while we only went *out* about once a week; we'd come full circle.

We were shaking down into marriage.

She had a pretty good knack for cooking, for a rookie, or if she didn't, it was all right with me, I didn't notice the difference. Just having her across the table made the food seem swell.

The apartment was easy for her to handle, just one oversize room with bed- and pantry-alcoves. We left it pretty much as it was....

...I woke up about two o'clock in the morning, everything dead still. I wanted a drink of water, or told myself I did anyway. She was sound asleep, or seemed to be; never moved as I got up. I shucked on a robe, went to the tap, and ran a little water into a glass. But then I didn't drink it after all. I carried it over to the window with me and stood there holding it in my hand, looking down into the street.

The street was empty, and gun-metal-gloom in color. No one on it, nobody, nothing that moved. Not an eddy of dust, not a cat on the prowl. I don't know why, but that made it less quieting than if there had been. The switch in the traffic-light control box up on the corner gave a click in the stillness that was as loud as the fall of a loose handcuff.

Still holding the water, I turned around and came back to the bed. Without moving, without changing position at all, she asked through closed eyes and all: "Anyone there?"

"No," I answered tersely, and got back to bed.

There was this tiny fist-sized cloud on the horizon now, no more than that.

But a tiny fist-sized cloud can mean a storm is coming, looming and monstrous.

...She was just lying there, on top of the bed, on top of the covers, face down. Still, but I knew she wasn't sleeping. I couldn't see her face, but I knew she wasn't crying either. She was sullenly smouldering. And it wasn't the neglected cigarette alongside her on the edge of a tray, spelling out its self-combustion in a weeping-willow strand of gray, that gave me the image alone. Smouldering was expressed in every turn, every line, of her limp, prostrate, quiescent, *waiting* body. Almost quivering with waiting and with smouldering, although it didn't move....

There was only one answer, one possible, inevitable, implicit answer, and I gave it to her. I gave her the answer that cinched it, the answer that clinched it, the answer that wrapped it up.

I raised my eyes, and looked up into the middle of her laughter, and asked: "Then what do you want me for?"

Her laughter crumbled away and died. She sat down suddenly, as though a spring had broken. She never did answer me at all from first to last, never gave me any answer. All she did was pinch the bridge of her nose tightly between her fingers as though it hurt her there, and crush her eyes closed hard. All she said was "Oh, God!" and shuddered all over, as though she felt cold, and as though she felt old, and as though she felt lonely.

Part 2
Ending

I was only trying to cheat death. I was only trying to surmount for a little while the darkness that all my life I surely knew was going to come rolling in on me some day and obliterate me. I was only trying to stay alive a brief while longer, after I was already gone. To stay in the light, to be with the living, a little while past my time. I loved them both so. A fool and his machine. Yes, a fool and his machine.

—a fragment from Woolrich's
notes for *Blues of a Lifetime*